About the authors

Giles Mohan is professor of international development at the Open University. He is a human geographer and studies African governance and the transnational connections to and from Africa, especially migrants. His recent work focuses on China's engagement with Africa and has been funded by a series of grants from the Economic and Social Research Council. He has published extensively in geographical, development studies and African studies journals and has acted as a consultant for a range of BBC documentaries on issues of international development.

Ben Lampert is a lecturer in the Development Policy and Practice Group at the Open University. He has a background in human geography and his research is concerned with the role of migrants and diaspora communities in development in Africa. His most recent work has been on Chinese migrants in Ghana and Nigeria.

May Tan-Mullins is a human geographer at the University of Nottingham Ningbo, China, having previously worked at the National University of Singapore and Durham University. Her research is concerned with environmental security and the political ecology of marine resources. Her most recent project concerns developmental debates and the politics of Chinese engagement with African development, and environmental and food security issues in China.

Daphne Chang is a staff tutor and a faculty associate of the Development Policy and Practice Group at the Open University. She is a social anthropologist. Her PhD research investigated the intermarriage of the Maasai and the Kikuyu in Kenya. Her recent work focuses on the lives and work of Chinese women migrants in Africa and the gender roles/relationships in Chinese family businesses in Africa.

CHINESE MIGRANTS AND AFRICA'S DEVELOPMENT

NEW IMPERIALISTS OR AGENTS OF CHANGE?

Giles Mohan, Ben Lampert, May Tan-Mullins and Daphne Chang

Zed Books
LONDON

Chinese Migrants and Africa's Development: New imperialists or agents of change? was first published in 2014 by Zed Books Ltd, 7 Cynthia Street, London N1 9JF, UK

www.zedbooks.co.uk

Set in Monotype Plantin and FFKievit by Ewan Smith, London NW5
Index: ed.emery@thefreeuniversity.net
Cover design: www.roguefour.co.uk
Cover images: Dar Es Salaam skyline © Frederic Courbet/Panos; construction workers © Mark Henley/Panos
Printed and bound by CPI Group (UK) Ltd, Croydon, CR0 4YY

A catalogue record for this book is available from the British Library
Library of Congress Cataloging in Publication Data available

ISBN 978-1-78032-917-8 hb
ISBN 978-1-78032-916-1 pb

CONTENTS

ABBREVIATIONS

ESRC   Economic and Social Research Council
FDI   foreign direct investment
FOCAC   Forum on China–Africa Cooperation
GIPC   Ghana Investment Promotion Centre
GUTA   Ghana Union of Traders' Associations
ICT   information and communications technology
MAN   Manufacturers Association of Nigeria
NGN   Nigerian naira
NLC   Nigeria Labour Congress
NUCFRLNMPE   National Union of Chemical, Footwear, Rubber,
        Leather and Non-Metallic Products Employees
PRC   People's Republic of China
RMB   renminbi
ROC   Republic of China
SEZ   Special Economic Zone
SMEs   small and medium-sized enterprises
SOE   state-owned enterprise

1 | THE CHINESE IN AFRICA: MIGRATION AND DEVELOPMENT BEYOND THE WEST

Introduction: African globalization and the emergence of China in Africa

Much of the discussion of China in Africa has been framed by oppositional discourses, which argue that the presence of Chinese people and firms is either uniformly 'bad' for Africans or resoundingly a 'good' thing. The most common of these are China's presence as a form of imperialism versus 'South–South' cooperation, large-scale importation of Chinese labour versus skills transfer, and exacerbating poor governance versus non-interference in sovereign states. These are important debates and ultimately link to big questions of change in the global order and the ideological perspectives of the powerful states involved. Yet, global restructuring and shifting power relations – the stuff of international relations and political economy – do not take place in the abstract. These changing relationships are about people on the move and the linkages between places, and so migration is central to them.

For much of the last century, when we think of foreign powers engaged in Africa we usually default to 'the West'. It is those European powers that colonized the continent, multinational corporations from the developed world, or the powerful US-based financial institutions which are seen as the key external actors engaging in Africa's (under) development. However, with the economic and political rise of a group of Asian countries, Brazil, Russia and a number of Middle Eastern states, the map of external intervention in Africa has grown massively more complex in the past decade. And accompanying these global shifts are migration flows of diplomats, traders, spouses, aid workers, students, tourists and construction workers. While African cities have always been cosmopolitan spaces, it is now common to see and hear an even greater diversity of peoples from across the globe.

It is the presence of China as a geopolitical actor and as a source of migrants that has provoked most attention, with claims that there are now as many as a million Chinese people living and working on the continent. In the twenty-five years that we have been research-ing in Africa, these growing Chinese connections have been very apparent. In many of the urban centres of southern Nigeria, if, as a Caucasian, you walk down the street, more often than not someone will shout *Oyibo*, the Nigerian Pidgin word meaning white person or foreigner. During fieldwork for this book in 2010, one of us, a white British male, was, for the first time, referred to in a similar street encounter in Lagos as *Chinko*, a somewhat disparaging reference to Chinese-made products which has also gained traction in both Ghana and Nigeria as a term for Chinese people. The rise of this expression reveals how commonplace it is to see people of East Asian origin on the streets and beaches and in the bars and shops of African cities. In our survey in Nigeria and Ghana, which we outline later in this chapter, around 75 per cent of respondents noted an increase in the number of Chinese people over the past five years. Moreover, the entry of *Chinko* into West African parlance attests to a profound sense of cultural difference that we will explore in this book.

Hence this book takes seriously Alden's (2007: 128) observation: 'The behaviour of thousands of newly settled Chinese businessmen and the conduct of the African communities in which they live and work will matter as much as the diplomacy and concessions made at the government level.' The book asks what does this migration mean for both the increasing number of Chinese migrants and their African 'hosts'? And how does this make us rethink the relationship between these new migration flows and development more broadly? The rest of this chapter addresses our major themes and the theoretical ap-proaches we have used to try and understand them. In both cases we often highlight the most salient aspects and in the substantive chapters we explore these themes and theories in more depth as they help illuminate our empirical analysis. In this chapter we also outline our methodology and data collection, which has unfolded over five years and across four African countries.

The state of knowledge and the book's themes

As with our opening observation, the migration and development issue has also been subject to a heated debate that tends to reflect ideological standpoints as opposed to a focused engagement with reality. A starting point for assessing the reality is the number of migrants.

Dubious data While most observers accept that China has sent an increased number of workers to Africa, particularly in the last decade, a major problem in assessing these migration flows is that data are speculative. Table 1.1 sets out some of the estimates for a range of historical periods up to the present.

Notwithstanding the serious limitations of such data, they lend themselves to several interpretations. First, the data show that sizeable, long-standing Chinese migrant communities in South Africa and Mauritius date back to the colonial period and that more recent immigration consisted of 1980s arrivals from Hong Kong and Taiwan. Second, the data also show that the rapid increases in Chinese immigration to Africa over the past decade coincide not only with China's increased foreign direct investment (FDI) but also with China's trade with various African countries. Mung (2008) estimated the current number of Chinese workers in Africa to be within the range of 270,000 to 510,000 and in 2007 the Xinhua Press Agency estimated that as many as 750,000 Chinese might be working or living in Africa for extended periods (cited in French and Polgreen 2007). As noted above, more recent estimates now put the figure at around a million. Whatever the general picture for Africa, the greatest growth is found in countries with significant oil resources, notably Nigeria, Angola and Sudan.

This paucity of data highlights three further issues that need to be considered in any study of the Chinese in Africa. First, history matters in terms of understanding the periodization of migration and its relationship to geopolitical forces, which we discuss in Chapters 2 and 3. In turn, this shapes the second issue: we must have a sharper focus on the social and geographical characteristics of migrants. Third, and related to the earlier issue, is the question of context.

TABLE 1.1 Estimates of the number of Chinese people in selected African countries

Country	1901–10 (Li 2000)	1940–50 (Li 2000)	1968 (Chang 1968)	1995 (Li 2000)	Estimate for 2003–07 (Sautman and Hairong 2007 and various sources)	2010–13 (various sources)
Mauritius		10,882	23,266	38,000	30,000 (2005)	30,000 (2010, www.tianya.cn)
Angola			500	300		260,000 (2012, news.163.com – Angola government)
Liberia			27	120	600 (2006)	
Madagascar	2,500	5,378	8,907	27,000	40,000 (2006,中国侨网; He 2009)	50,000 (2010, www.tianya.cn)
South Africa	70,000	4,153	5,105	27,515	100,000–400,000 (2007)	350,000 (2012, news.163.com – South Africa police)
Ethiopia			18	55	3,000–4,000 (2006)	
Réunion	2,500	3,853	3,000	20,000–25,000 (1972)		20,000 (2010, www.tianya.cn)
Mozambique	500		1,735	600	1,500 (2006)	

					Source
Cameroon		3	407	1,000–3,000 (2005)	20,000 (2010, news.163.com – Cameroon reporter)
Nigeria	4	2	5,100	100,000 (2007)	150,000 (2010, www.tianya.cn)
Egypt	64	27	110	5,000–10,000 (2004–05)	100,000 (2010, news.163.com – Egypt independent post)
Sudan		N/A	45		30,000 (2011, news.163.com – Yale dissertation)
Ghana			700	6,000 (2004)	6,000–10,000 (Marfaing and Thiel 2011)
Zimbabwe		303	500	10,000 (2007)	50,000 (2010, www.tianya.cn)
Tanzania					10,000 (2011, news.163.com – Tanzania Chinese chamber of commerce)
Total in Africa	26,899	43,734		550,000 (2007, Zhang and Wang 2010: 7)	1,000,000 (estimates, Park 2009; Zhang and Wang 2010, www.tianya.cn)

As diasporas are bound by ethnic sameness, however fictitious, but dwell in multiple places, it is difficult to speak of a singular diasporic identity. So, a further issue is how space and place affect the nature of the Chinese migrant community and their developmental potential – something we return to below.

Ideological divisions Assessing the significance and impact of Chinese migrants is not just a function of data or the accuracy of the 'facts' we assemble. Playing into this are ideological debates about how we understand and interpret change. A recent example of such polarized debate concerns Chinese copper mines in Zambia where there have been a number of industrial problems over the past decade that have attracted international media coverage. Moreover, the issue has been scrutinized by Zambian and international civil society organizations (Fraser and Lungu 2007; Human Rights Watch 2011) which paint a picture of Chinese firms as the worst in terms of pay, labour conditions and workers' rights. In a rebuttal to some of these claims, Yan and Sautman (2013) produced data that suggest Chinese firms are no worse than non-Chinese firms and that the critique of these firms functions to paint western interests in a better light. Indeed, to claim that Chinese firms are 'worse' requires some kind of comparative analysis against which Chinese performance can be judged, but in most of these negative portrayals of China, Yan and Sautman argue, such a comparison was lacking.

Playing into these ideological and methodological problems are disciplinary divides that hinder a rounded understanding of the migration issue, so we develop a more interdisciplinary analysis of everyday China–Africa relations, drawing on economic sociology, human geography, anthropology, political science and gender studies. Most work on China in Africa has been economistic, focusing on trade, aid and investment flows, sometimes augmented by a case study or two (e.g. Power et al. 2012; Fessahaie and Morris 2013). There have been some analyses of the politics of these relations, but politics tends to be the formal arena of inter-state diplomacy and so focuses on elite actors in and around the state (e.g. Large 2009; Carmody et al. 2012; Holslag 2011). There have been some attempts to disaggregate the state with commentary on the ways that street-level bureaucrats in Africa seek advantage from Chinese businesses (e.g. Dobler 2008) or the regulatory weaknesses of particular African ministries in relation to Chinese firms (e.g. Haglund 2009). Relatively little work has been done on the engagement with China by civil society actors in Africa beyond a handful of studies on trade unions (e.g. Lee 2009; Baah and Jauch 2009) and business associations (e.g. Lee 2007).

In contrast to these economic and political analyses there is a small but growing body of work on the social and cultural under-pinnings of the relationships between Chinese migrants in Africa and, increasingly, African migrants in China (e.g. Monson 2009; Hsu 2007; Haugen and Carling 2005; Bodomo 2010; Bredeloup 2012; Giese and Thiel 2012; Mohan and Lampert 2013). There is also some work on African attitudes to China and the Chinese (e.g. Sautman and Yan 2009; Ngome 2009; Shen and Taylor 2012) and Chinese attitudes to-wards Africa and Africans (Shen 2009; McNamee et al. 2012). These are proving invaluable for giving greater nuance to broad-brush claims about 'China' and 'Africa', though many of them lack an explicit theory of cultural encounter or exchange, or how these cultural relationships play into the political economy of development. This is changing (e.g. Ayers 2012), but much more work could be done on trying to integrate political economy with more culturally sensitive accounts (see Meagher 2012). A significant gap – the gender dynamics of China–Africa relations – exists in this work and this is something we explicitly address in this book.

We will be visiting these and other studies throughout the book but some of the key themes they reveal are as follows. First, there is general approval of the Chinese presence in Africa by Africans. Ngome's (2009) attitude survey in Cameroon suggests that although 70 per cent of respondents were concerned about the growing number of Chinese, 81 per cent welcomed Chinese products, 92 per cent felt the Chinese helped Cameroon's economy in some way, and 79 per cent recommended that relations between China and Cameroon continue, with some modifications. Sautman and Yan's (2009) survey across nine African countries focused on university students and faculty instead of a broad demographic cross-section of Africans. In general, respondents were positive about the role that Chinese small businesses played, they felt that the Chinese model of development was a good one, and were impressed by the work ethic of Chinese migrants. With regard to Zambia, Sautman and Yan contend that patterns of attitudes are similar across Africa.

Our own survey concurs with these findings with 42 per cent of Ghanaians and 54 per cent of Nigerians surveyed feeling that the Chinese had positive effects on them and their families, and 55 per cent in both countries felt their standard of living had increased as a result of the Chinese. Of those who had some contact with Chinese people, 55 per cent of Ghanaian respondents and 75 per cent of Nigerian respondents said they liked, admired or respected them. And thinking about the future, 43 per cent of Ghanaian and 56 per cent of Nigerian respondents felt China would be good for their respective countries. Asked why, the top answers for Ghana were 33 per cent more jobs, 23 per cent new skills, and 20 per cent new technology. Comparable responses for Nigeria were 36 per cent new technology and 28 per cent more jobs. Set against this for the 25 per cent of Ghanaians and 11 per cent of Nigerians surveyed who thought China would be bad for them in the future, the reasons were around 35 per cent taking resources, 25 per cent flooding markets, and 16 per cent taking jobs.

However, our survey findings, which we introduce throughout the book as appropriate, qualify this acceptance in various ways. For example, where concerns were raised about such things as taxation or job creation, it was generally noted that these were as much matters for the host African states to sort out, as they were something unique to the way Chinese migrants acted. Second, having said this, there has been a politicization of the presence of Chinese migrants by some African political actors in tandem with the over-reporting of such incidents in the western press. We noted the case of Zambia where the international press has picked up on strained industrial relations. Sautman and Yan (2009) argue that where strongly negative sentiments emerge, influential political leaders quite often stoke these tensions, something we discuss in Chapter 5. Civil society actors have engaged with the Chinese presence, often in relation to business competition, wages and industrial relations. In some cases we have seen positive outcomes of such campaigning, as in the case of Ghana's TUC getting recognition for the union at Sinohydro's Bui Dam site, but in other cases the weakness of the trade unions and the determination of certain political elites has meant that the Chinese are relatively favoured in negotiations (Lee 2009).

In terms of social and spatial relations, a third finding from the existing literature is that Chinese migrants often, for various reasons, stay relatively isolated from the African societies where they reside. The nature of this relative isolation depends on the type of firm and the nature of its business. In the case of Chinese state-owned enterprises (SOEs), we see Chinese technicians and labourers living in compounds adjacent to the construction site; and some other larger firms provide purpose-built accommodation for their staff. We also see China Towns in larger African cities, which are mainly dedicated retail spaces, sometimes with living accommodation above the shop premises. Playing into some of this social segregation is a sense of 'threat' from Africans. Chinese respondents in various studies, including our own, reported incidents of crime against them, which they used to explain their self-imposed distance from the locals. Playing into this there is for many a profound sense of cultural difference on both sides of the 'China' and 'Africa' divide, with language often acting as a barrier to further mutual understanding. That said, and this is the fourth issue, the idea of 'enclaved' Chinese communities is partial and we see significant mixing across the cultures in particular contexts. In the case of small and medium-sized enterprises (SMEs) the Chinese owners and managers are forced to engage directly with Africans as employees, customers or partners. And it is in these relationships that we often see agency on the part of Africans in leveraging benefits from the Chinese presence. Fifth, and finally, existing studies show that divisions exist within 'the Chinese' migrant communities on issues such as length of time away from China, source region, gender and social class. Such findings caution us against those readings of Chinese business organization that reduce them to some essential feature of Chinese culture.

These existing studies have proven invaluable in beginning to go beyond the polarized debates that we noted at the start of this chapter. Using these studies as a starting point, here we set out three broad agendas that we pick up in this book. Many of the arguments 'for' or 'against' China's role in Africa tend to be based on essentialist and ideologically driven assumptions about 'China' and 'Africa' as well as particular ways of reading the political economy of development. The first main theme we explore in this book is the tension between structure and culture. Much of the critique in the Zambia example, which is emblematic of the wider China-in-Africa discourse, is based on something unique about 'Chinese culture' and the idea that 'they' do things in a particularly exploitative way. By failing to compare Chinese firms with other international firms, or Zambian ones for that matter, the analysis obscures the structural way in which the Zambian economy and Zambian workers are exploited by foreign capital. An ambition of this book is to move beyond culturalist explanations and reinsert a critical political economy of capitalist accumulation into the analysis (see Ayers 2012), which is attentive to class exploitation and the intersection of class with other axes of social difference rather than focus on cultural difference per se.

The second theme we explore builds on this need for a disaggregated political economy and concerns the methodological nationalism of most studies. Methodological nationalism refers to the tendency to see nation-states as the natural containers for social processes, in which there is a congruence of social, political and economic borders. As Ayers (ibid.) observed, most studies of China and Africa are state-centric and many of the studies of the politics of these relationships focus on bilateral elite relations. There is also the broader issue of focusing on undifferentiated national cultural groupings such that many studies tend to be about 'the Chinese' in African country 'x' and rarely disaggregate the different flows of Chinese migrants. While we agree that strict methodological nationalism is unhelpful given the networked nature of many transnational flows, it is also the case that states matter as actors, and discourses of statehood and feelings of national identity are also meaningful for many actors. Hence, our book seeks to capture the state-based, inter-state and extra-state connections of everyday China–Africa encounters. Part of this is to adopt a multiple country approach, which we discuss presently, as a way of seeing how far local context affects the ways in which these complex relationships play out.

The third theme for our book builds on this issue of context and social action. In most cases of western journalism (and much academic debate), 'the Chinese' are assumed to drive the relationship whereas in Chinese reporting (and many official academic sources) it is a 'win–win' relationship that benefits both China and Africa. In Africa, the picture is more mixed depending on the interests of who is speaking. For example, African trade associations often see China as a threat to African firms and jobs, whereas African political elites publicly welcome the loans and infrastructure the Chinese bring, given that they can enhance their regime's legitimacy by providing tangible evidence of 'development'. But the focus on China as the 'driver' of these relationships at the expense of a 'passive' Africa repeats long-standing ways of portraying Africa and Africans (Mudimbe 1988). In such representations Africa is at the whim of external forces, which belies a deeper racist assumption about the inability of Africans to fashion their own destiny. So, through a relational understanding of Chinese and Africans our book seeks to foreground African agency. This, then, produces a much more mixed view of how China in Africa plays out.

Theories of 'South–South' migration

As we are concerned with a more interdisciplinary understanding of structure and agency in accounts of Chinese migration to Africa, then, our study is situated within wider framings of migration and development and here we set up the key theoretical concepts that frame subsequent chapters. We begin by looking at political economy accounts of migration that hold on to the ways these changes are driven and experienced by individuals. To understand social mixing we use ideas of conviviality, which are useful but empirically underdeveloped. Likewise, we are interested in complex subject positions and so use work on intersectionality to try and hold on to multiple and shifting senses of identity.

Migration, globalization and social transformation In seeking to
analyse Chinese migrants in Africa in relational and developmental
terms, we use Castles' (2009; 2010) analysis of migration and development as *social transformation*. The attraction of this framework is that
it moves away from the methodological nationalism that pervades
much of the work on migration and, in contrast to the 'sedentarist
bias', treats migration as normal and constitutive of social change.
The sedentarist bias assumes that people aspire to a fixed base in
a particular locality and that 'normal' development works through
such fixity. By seeing migration and mobility as constitutive of social
transformation, we move away from viewing it as an aberration which
needs to be 'managed' for development.

Under globalization and neoliberalism (Hoogvelt 1997), the
deepening of capitalist relations over many decades intensifies the
processes of transformation across space such that actions in developed countries have direct impacts on less developed countries,
one of which, according to Castles, is 'South' to 'North' migration.
For African societies, globalization is a long-standing reality and as
Ferguson (2006) argues it has re-emphasized Africa's position in the
global economy as a supplier of raw materials, but this is no longer
attached to a Keynesian discourse of national development. Rather,
it is tied to a free-market individualism where the state takes a min-
imalist role in social protection. It is also a process that entrenches
the power of elites who can control access to these resources, which
is where, as noted, much of the political analysis of China in Africa
has focused (see Carmody 2011).

This broad framing of global restructuring is important but
misses two crucial elements. First, the rise of China is now a major
part of the globalization story (e.g. Henderson 2008; Jacques 2009)
and has been for a long time. As such, the globalization narrative
is premised on an assumed western-centredness rather than on a
longer and more multi-nodal process of globalization (King 1991),
which dates back to at least the mercantile and colonial eras. In
turn, the rise of China and other 'new' world powers adds new
actors to the African economic landscape without necessarily changing the terms on which this occurs (Ayers 2012). The result is that

migration flows are not simply South to North, but South to South (see Mohan 2013).

China's development is part of this wider restructuring that involves a form of what Harvey (2003) characterizes as the revitalization of primitive accumulation. Far from this 'accumulation by dispossession' being a temporary feature of capitalism, it is an incomplete and recurring phenomenon, given new legitimacy under neoliberalism in which displacement of people and a violent proletarianization are the norm for many in the developing world (Ayers 2012; Bush et al. 2011). This moves us away from considering China as a bounded actor and for our purposes situates the China–Africa relationship as constituted from a series of interconnected transformations, not least the movement of global production to South East Asia from the late 1970s, the opening up of African economies during the structural adjustment programmes of the 1980s and growing western indebtedness.

However, by situating China in 'the context of a significant spatial reorganization of global capitalism' (Ayers 2012: 13) we cannot simply read off Chinese activities in Africa from an abstract 'reorganization' thesis, but need to account for how specific actors and discourses on the Chinese side and more widely enable these specific activities to come into being. This is echoed in Castles' comment that some approaches to transformation are essentially top-down and 'fail to analyse the local effects of global economic and political forces' (2009: 16). That said, the Chinese firms central to its internationalization are capitalist and so we have to acknowledge the accumulation imperative in any relationship with African actors.

China's 'state-orchestrated market capitalism' (Ampiah and Naidu 2008: 330) has produced consistently high growth for two decades, but energy security is required to sustain this growth. China has therefore been forced to look beyond its borders for sources of energy and other natural resources, as well as for new markets and geopolitical influence. This resulted in China's Going Out strategy and its 'Africa policy' whereby China encouraged outward investment by subsidizing it, offering financial support, information dissemination, tax incentives, credit and loans. While this primarily benefited larger Chinese companies, particularly SOEs, smaller private firms have also been supported by these policies. As such, China's outward investment is similar to that of other nations; the international business literature (Dunning and Lundan 2008) identifies four major sets of motives – resource seeking (for example, commodities), market accessing (a market for sales or construction contracts), cost reducing (for example, low labour costs) and asset augmenting (learning new skills or access to new technology). China's motives primarily cover the first two of these, although some argue that doing business in Africa is seen as the first step in learning the ropes of international business.

Second, while globalization is seen to concern transnational firms, inter-state negotiations, and multilateral institutions, it is also about small firms which may operate outside any obvious state-based agendas; what some have referred to as 'globalization from below' (Portes 1997) or 'low-end globalization' (Mathews and Yang 2012). In the context of China in Africa, much debate has focused on resource-accessing and market-seeking state-backed FDI projects which we noted tend to be quite enclavic. As a result, analysis has, until recently, ignored the actions of small, independent, market-accessing firms. Private Chinese firms are increasingly significant and it is estimated that around 85 per cent of Chinese companies investing in Africa are privately owned (Gu 2009). These companies are driven by 'African market opportunities, competition within China and the presence of a strong entrepreneurial spirit' (ibid.: 570). While we have to avoid endowing Chinese business people with some essential 'spirit', it is true that the businesses participating in this lower end globalization operate at the frontiers of new markets. These frontiers may be former communist states or countries with recently existing civil strife, but the common thread is riskiness and more adverse operating environments. While a few large privately owned companies such as Huawei Technologies, Holley Group and Zhongxing ZTE Corporation have operations in Africa, the majority of these private firms are SMEs. Most of these companies were motivated to invest overseas because of access to larger markets in comparison with the highly competitive domestic markets, which also have production surpluses.

Hence, there are different modes and scales over which globalization occurs. Here we are inspired by Anna Tsing's idea of 'friction' in which global connections can only 'be charged and enacted in the sticky materiality of practical encounters' (Tsing 2004: 1), which produces unexpected and sometimes contradictory effects. In this vein Castles argues for a multi-scaled analysis that simultaneously connects analysis at global, national and local levels. This is not only sensitive to historical conditioning but also to the local context, which is partly about political institutions and also about human agency. He notes: 'Social transformation processes are mediated by local historical and cultural patterns, through which people develop varying forms of agency and resistance' (2010: 1576). Castles' multi-scaled approach echoes Mung's (2008) analysis of the Chinese in Africa which talks about the need for a 'triangular' analysis that tracks relations between China, the Chinese in Africa, and the relationships between the Chinese in Africa and Africans.

We noted earlier that while we want to avoid a rigid methodological nationalism we still see states as significant. One implication of the multi-scaled approach suggested by Castles is that states still matter as the building blocks of the international system and they have determining effects on mobilities of various sorts. Certainly the attitude of the Chinese state towards out-migration has shifted a number of times in the last 150 years (something we discuss in the next chapter) while African states have used the entry of China as a way of playing 'old' powers off against these 'newer' ones. But politics exists beyond the state and in our analysis of Chinese migrants in West Africa we examine popular agency and resistance (see Mohan and Lampert 2013), which helps us understand both the tensions and conviviality we see.

Cosmopolitanism, conviviality and intersectionality One way to undertake the 'triangulation' that Mung urges is through rather abstract notions of cosmopolitanism, hospitality and conviviality (see Jazeel 2011). The value of such an endeavour is to move beyond fixed notions of identity and to explore the ways in which interaction and mixing occur. While a detailed discussion of these concepts is beyond the scope of this chapter, questions of cosmopolitan dispositions

(Knowles 2007) and everyday encounters are germane to our discussion.

Certain cosmopolitan values and practices (Vertovec and Cohen 2002) of openness and experimentation are evident in the way that Chinese and Africans engage and these 'subaltern cosmopolitanisms' (Gidwani 2006) usefully shift our focus from the assumed agents of such values: namely, enlightened western males. Moreover, while the idea of convivial social relations has been posited by Gilroy (2004) as a real and useful antidote to a postcolonial 'melancholia' in the UK, it remains an empirically lifeless concept (Bonnett 2010) and we discuss its use in more detail in Chapter 6.

Methodologically, conviviality points us to the 'ethnography of the ordinary' (Overing and Passes 2000: 8), which echoes Castles' call to examine the 'local effects' of globalization. It also echoes recent work in diaspora and development, which has sought to shift away from the focus on remittances and/or diaspora organizations as the ways in which diasporas support development. Page and Mercer (2012) argue that the remittances discourse has come to dominate the migration and development literature and in so doing cements a model of development based on rationalizing individuals. In contrast, these authors argue that we need to focus on a broader range of 'social practices' that migrants engage in through which we might get a richer picture of what 'development' in or by the diaspora looks like. Certainly, an ambition of this book is to avoid the assumption, implicit in so much commentary, that 'the Chinese' have singularly economic agendas and, as such, very one-dimensional subjectivity. We want to examine migrants as diverse, complex and contradictory.

Here we break away from fixed and homogenizing understandings of classes and tease out the interplay of structured economic relationships with other axes of social identity (e.g. Gibson-Graham 2006). Much of the literature on Chinese business has taken a Weberian line (Portes and Sensenbrenner 1993), which we find problematic and which is something we examine in detail in Chapter 4. Much of the Weberian inspired embeddedness literature on Chinese firms tends to posit cultural closure and the essentializing of 'groups' (Meagher 2012; Greenhalgh 1994). Here we get closed communities and 'ethnic' economies built around *guanxi*. As Meagher and Greenhalgh argue, 'Confucian' values often mask an invidious exploitation of 'unfree' family labour dating back to the colonial period which was, to some extent, a survival strategy for Chinese firms in the face of unfair European practices (Li 2012).

Such a critique of ideal-typical Confucian capitalism urges us to examine concrete practices on the ground. Meagher (2012) argues that Chinese firms can play a brokerage role between enterprises. Here she uses Bräutigam's (2003) work on 'flying geese industrialization' where the Chinese presence can kick-start local economic development. By contrast, when Meagher takes Hart's (1996) work on South Africa and Taiwan, we get a different reading and an analysis closer to Lee's (2009) political economy about casualization and undercutting, which is anything but developmental. Meagher usefully argues that when Chinese networks 'touch ground' in Africa – echoing Tsing's (2004) friction – they become more like African networks. By this she means that in the period after independence Chinese firms enjoyed supportive and regularized relations with African states, but more recently newly arriving firms encounter a less supportive environment and enter various 'irregular activities' such as illegal foreign exchange transactions and bribery.

The general context for this debate about culture and business is one of explaining capitalist variation. At its heart is a debate about whether capitalism is constituted of transhistorical and universal components or whether meaningful differences are evident in the nature of multiple capitalisms. The 'varieties of capitalism' debate (Peck and Theodore 2007) refers to Weberian approaches seeking to understand the differences that institutions make to the organization and trajectory of different capitalisms that are understood to be nationally centred. Rather than explore this debate in detail, we follow Peck and Theodore's attempt to signal a 'variegated capitalism' approach that is not nationally centred. As Tsing (2004: 4) warns, 'There is no point in studying fully discrete "capitalisms"' because, due to the co-evolution of capitalism with multiple institutional assemblages, we see different forms of combined and uneven development under capitalism rather than multiple forms of capitalism (Rosenberg 2006).

This usefully points to a contextual understanding of the relationship between class, cultural capital and ethnicity (Ellis 2011) and their connection to development impacts. That said, the smaller Chinese firms we examine are capitalist and so we have to acknowledge the accumulation imperative in any relationship with African actors and the possibility of exclusion, marginalization and exploitation. Such interplay of multiple social differences can be captured in the idea of intersectionality. Largely coming out of critical race and gender studies, it refers to 'the interaction between gender, race and other categories of difference in individual lives, social practices, institutional arrangements, and cultural ideologies and the outcomes of these interactions in terms of power' (Davis 2008: 68). It is not our intention to deal in detail with the various uses of intersectionality (see, e.g., McCall 2005: Davis 2008; Yuval-Davis 2006), but we find it a useful heuristic device for thinking through the ways in which the contextualized operation of multiple social categories play out, such that we cannot separate out any one as having causal or explanatory primacy. Chapter 5 develops our use of intersectionality.

Picking up on various strands in intersectional theory, the notion of context is important. Many social theorists historicize this context such that older, possibly extant processes of subjectification may condition certain present-day positionings. Or they may make comparative parallels with previous times. Equally important is the spatiality of intersections. If we are to explore Yuval-Davis's idea of different ontologies coming together in specific contexts, then we have to understand place-based processes of political, economic and cultural positioning. Valentine's work (2007) focuses on the experiential aspects of intersectionality, which is fluid and malleable. It changes in different spaces and in relation to those occupying those spaces such that the same person in one space may be subject to very different powerful positionings and openings in another.

Methodology: qualitative, quantitative and comparative

Picking up on the need to examine context comparatively, here we set out the research design from which many of the data derive. This book arose out of a series of projects, mostly funded by the

UK's Economic and Social Research Council (ESRC). The research is organized around two primary case studies of Nigeria and Ghana, with some other data from Angola and Tanzania plus academic studies and news reports from other contexts.

In order to capture the structural forces and individual agency, we utilized a mixed methodology (Findlay and Li 1999). Qualitative case studies were used, because local context matters to the process of migrant interaction and integration and we were keen to analyse causal processes linking economic, social and political factors. Our first project from 2007 to 2010 collected forty-two interviews with Chinese migrants in Ghana and Angola, which were conducted in Mandarin by Dr Tan-Mullins, a Singaporean national of Chinese origin. Most of these were entrepreneurs in small firms though some were working for aid projects. There were also around forty interviews with Ghanaians and other expatriates involved in working with the Chinese or developing policies concerned with inward investment. The second project ran from 2010 to 2012 and focused on Ghana and Nigeria. We conducted 102 interviews with Chinese migrants, mostly in SMEs but some were part of larger, Chinese state-backed investment projects and private Chinese transnational corporations. These were conducted in English and Mandarin by Dr Lampert using the networking and translations skills of a Chinese-speaking Nigerian researcher who had worked extensively with Chinese firms in West Africa. We also undertook sixty-one interviews with Nigerians and Ghanaians connected to or affected by the Chinese presence, such as employers of Chinese labour or capital goods, employees of Chinese companies, local competitors, government officials, trade unions and so on.

Part of the second project also involved a survey of local attitudes to the Chinese presence (Schuman and Presser 1996). The reason for this was to move away from viewing the Chinese migrants in isolation and to avoid characterizing their interactions with Africans to instances of 'exploitation' or 'tension'. The survey enabled us to garner more variegated perceptions of the Chinese presence. The surveys were conducted among a sample of 1,084 Ghanaians and 600 Nigerians, from which we conducted a further sixty in-depth

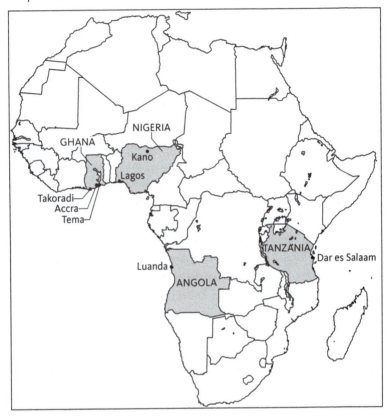

Map 1.1 African case study countries and fieldwork locations

follow-up interviews. The final piece of research undertaken by Dr Chang was an adjunct to the latter project and she focused on female migrants in Nigeria and Tanzania. This was a smaller pilot project and involved eighteen in-depth interviews in Nigeria and participant observation in Tanzania. The Nigeria interviews were with independent female migrants and drew from the larger sample of the ESRC project. While the book is based principally on our primary data, it will also draw on examples and data from other studies and so we address other parts of Africa.

The case study countries were selected for the similarities and differences they offer in terms of the issues under investigation. In Nigeria the Chinese population is estimated at between 100,000 and

150,000 and in Ghana between 7,000 and 20,000. In both countries the Chinese are concentrated in the major commercial cities and the oil-producing areas though we find increasing numbers in rural areas as traders and working in semi-legal resource extraction. In both countries there is evidence of Chinese networks dating back to the late 1950s, most of which originated in Hong Kong (Ho 2008; Utomi 2008).

In all countries there is a growing Chinese presence in retail, small-scale manufacturing, services and infrastructure, which allowed comparative analysis of these sectors (Colombant 2006; Okere 2006). The strong presence in retail allowed us to compare the perceptions of Nigerians and Ghanaians to the commodity trade the Chinese bring. Moreover, the Chinese are establishing two of the five Special Economic Zones (SEZs) designated for sub-Saharan Africa in Nigeria (Bräutigam and Tang 2011), though the total is seven for Africa when the north of the continent is included. By contrast, Ghana lacks sizeable strategic mineral resources – although oil has recently been discovered (McCaskie 2008) – and here the Chinese presence is mainly in light manufacturing (e.g. enamelware), infrastructure (e.g. the Bui Dam) and trade, all of which ostensibly 'benefit' a wide section of society. A growing trend has been for Chinese migrants to engage in illegal gold mining – known locally as *galamsey* – which has become something of a sore point in China–Ghana relations (Hirsch 2013). Both countries are former British colonies with English as one of the official languages. However, Nigeria is a much larger federation with well-organized ethnic political blocs (Beckman 1982; Watts 1994), and these have determined the direction of spending of oil revenue. While Ghana is ethnically diverse, it is smaller and arguably less ethnicized in its politics (Lentz and Nugent 2000). Ghana has since independence been regarded by the Chinese as an ideological leader in West Africa, which has affected the levels of Chinese aid (Weinstein 1975). These differences in the relationship between the state, ethnicity and resources are used to explore the different reception given to the Chinese.

Within each country two localities were selected on the basis of the different nature of their Chinese communities and their relationships to local society. In Nigeria, we focused on Lagos and Kano. The former is located on the coast in the south-west corner of Nigeria and is the country's largest city, main port and principal commercial and industrial centre. It is also the pre-eminent hub of the Chinese presence in the country with a diverse range of Chinese entrepreneurial and corporate activities. It is home to the largest concentration of Chinese traders, most visibly symbolized by the strikingly red-walled China Town shopping complex in Ojota on the eastern edge of the city. This officially opened in 2005 after a gradual relocation from its original site in Ikoyi, where it was first established in 1999. Specializing in the retail and wholesale of affordable consumer goods such as clothes and household items, the complex still attracts customers and traders from across Nigeria, despite a significant decline in its fortunes in recent years, as we discuss in Chapter 5. Some Chinese traders can also be found in and around local markets in the city, such as in a disused corporate tower block on the edge of Lagos Island's main market area, and there are several retail outlets established by Chinese companies that import, and sometimes assemble, products such as machinery, electrical goods and furniture.

Chinese enterprises are particularly prominent in Lagos's hospitality sector where they include hotels and guesthouses and, most notably, over a dozen Chinese restaurants, the largest and most exclusive of which are found in the upmarket Victoria Island district. Large state-owned and private Chinese companies operating in sectors such as oil, telecommunications and construction have substantial offices in Lagos and there is a significant Chinese presence in the manufacturing sector, with the two largest Hong Kong Chinese industrial groups in the country having major facilities in Ikeja and Ikorodu respectively, with a number of Hong Kong, Taiwanese and more recent mainland Chinese factories and assembly plants dotted across the city's industrial estates. And to the east of central Lagos, work is under way on the Lekki Free Trade Zone, a huge, Sino-Nigerian joint venture and one of the seven SEZs that China is supporting across Africa.

Kano is the largest city and main commercial and industrial

centre in the north of Nigeria, located on the fringes of the Sahel at the start of the historic trans-Sahara trade route. It is one of the principal centres of the Chinese population in Nigeria, and is probably second only to Lagos. It also has a long-standing, primarily Hong Kong-origin Chinese manufacturing presence and, alongside Ikorodu in Lagos, it is the main base of one of the two largest Hong Kong Chinese industrial conglomerates in the country, reportedly employing hundreds of Chinese workers alongside thousands of African workers in the city. The more recent wave of Chinese trading enterprises has also reached Kano, but here it is focused largely on the importation of textiles, with a number of wholesale outlets appearing on the perimeter of the city's famous textile market. As in Lagos, there is also a notable Chinese presence in the hospitality sector, with several Chinese restaurants, some of which are attached to guesthouses.

In Ghana, we focused our ethnographic research on Accra and Tema. Accra is the capital of Ghana and the country's largest city and main commercial centre. Like Lagos, it has attracted a highly visible Chinese trading presence, particularly around Rawlings Park in the central market area where, in the mid-2000s, a large complex was boldly branded as the 'Ghana Chinese Commodities Wholesale Town'. While only a few Chinese shops remain in this building, they are a prominent feature of the neighbouring side-streets and even dominate some smaller retail complexes in the area, where they offer a range of affordable goods including shoes, luggage, electrical fittings and household items. Accra is also the national headquarters for a number of Chinese SOEs and large private companies, with construction companies particularly well represented. The hospitality sector is again an area where there is a strong Chinese presence, with a good range of middle to high-end Chinese restaurants, which appear to be especially popular in Accra, and a couple of large, Chinese-owned hotels recently rising near the airport to make a prominent mark on the city's skyline.

While there are some Chinese factories in Accra, the greatest concentration is in Tema, an industrial and harbour complex built in the 1950s and early 1960s just to the east of the capital. Tema represents

Ghana's main industrial centre and Chinese companies have a notable and long-standing presence there, including established Hong Kong and Taiwanese textile, metal and plastic product manufacturers and some more recent mainland Chinese factories focusing on the likes of wood and metal working, plastic recycling and food processing. Alongside this are a number of other Chinese businesses such as a large hotel, beauty salon, acupuncture clinic, a sizeable state-owned fishing operation, a couple of Chinese supermarkets and several restaurants, some with guesthouses and/or casinos attached. We had also intended to study Sekondi-Takoradi, a port to the west which we thought would have attracted significant Chinese interest given that Ghana's new oil industry lies offshore. However, we found only a few Chinese businesses in the city, including one of the oldest surviving Hong Kong Chinese enamelware factories and a new, mid-range Chinese restaurant which had been enticed there by the prospect of servicing the oil industry. The Chinese presence is likely to have expanded further since our fieldwork, with the growth of the oil sector and work commencing on a large Chinese government-backed oil and gas 'infrastructure corridor'.

In Angola there was very little sign of Chinese migrants during the civil war period. It was only after 2002, when the war ended, that we began to see the opening of the country to foreign investment and migrants. Angola's growth was mainly fuelled by oil and natural resources exports, and with it a construction boom in the capital, Luanda. This brought in Chinese contractors on the back of 'oil-for-infrastructure' loans leading to a spike in the number of Chinese entering the country. The current estimate for the number of Chinese people in Angola is 260,000 (news.163.com 2012).

Our fieldwork in Angola between 2007 and 2011 found most multinational Chinese enterprises headquartered in Luanda. These enterprises were mainly large to medium sized, with Chinese state support, and were mostly in the construction sector. We also found a few service and trading companies, such as air ticketing, hotels, restaurants, import and export companies, and food and beverage manufacturers. In the main these catered to the expatriate Chinese and upper-class Angolan markets. In addition, there were some smaller enterprises and construction projects scattered beyond the capital city, such as ChangAn Construction Ltd and Anhui Angola Construction Company. As a Portuguese ex-colony, Angola presented another challenge for Chinese SMEs as there are additional costs in terms of translation services. This possibly explained why there were fewer small-scale enterprises in Angola compared with Nigeria and Ghana.

Dar es Salaam is the commercial centre of Tanzania, one of the hubs of transportation for the East Africa coast since AD 1000, as well as the largest city. Kariakoo Ward contains a large market sprawling over many streets and hosts a concentration of Chinese businesses. Chinese traders sell hardware, construction materials, plastic ware, kitchenware, curtains, locks and electronic appliances. Some of them also occupy apartment buildings as living quarters. Many shops selling construction materials have warehouses outside Kariakoo with customers able to pay for their goods in the Kariakoo shop and collect them from the warehouse. Chinese restaurants can be found all over the city, including in the most affluent area, Oysterbay. There are also a number of Chinese medicine practitioners in Dar es Salaam.

Accessing the respondents It had not been the intention in our first project to study small Chinese firms in any detail. Rather, we were concerned with the more formal state-level projects, either funded by Chinese aid or through some sort of commercial loan. It was the limited access to these major projects in Ghana that forced us to see if we could go through networks of smaller entrepreneurs who were easier to locate and talk to. This difficulty of accessing Chinese state institutions was not a surprise to us and is well documented in the literature (Heimer and Thogersen 2006). Research in China with the ministries and state-related enterprises was also difficult. In 2008, in an environment of western media criticism and the run-up to the Forum on China–Africa Cooperation (FOCAC) IV, we found officials quite defensive about inquiries into China's presence in Africa. The interviews were heavily shaped by an awareness of the negative media coverage about China in Africa (Mawdsley 2008). Hence, the process of access was heavily shaped by legacies of imperialism, Orientalism, bureaucratic practice and global media.

By comparison it was less problematic to talk to SOEs in Africa, particularly Angola, perhaps due to the 'distance' from the central authorities and party influences in China. That said, the atmosphere in the SOEs was still restrictive, with formal interview settings and several senior members of staff present. And like the fieldwork conducted in China, the information was very much the party line, emphasizing 'South–South' cooperation and 'mutual benefit'. Comparatively, it was easier to talk to the private enterprises, regardless of size, in Ghana, Nigeria and Angola. In Ghana, the SMEs provided rich information and people were very willing to share their experiences while in Angola, both the large enterprises and smaller SMEs were easy to access. Also, the relatively small size and insularity of many Chinese migrant networks makes it necessary to welcome the newcomers into their group, such as Dr Tan-Mullins, although her welcome may have also been due to the fact that she was not an obvious commercial threat to any of them. In Ghana and Nigeria, the community was older and more established than in Angola and as a result more cliquish and enclosed.

The plan to access the major projects through smaller firms was driven by our somewhat naïve belief in the totality of a 'Beijing Consensus' insofar as we assumed that a Chinese 'community' existed and that if we accessed it at one point it would not be hard to work our way through to where we wanted to be. In Ghana our strategy was to start at the Central Market in Accra where we knew some Chinese traders were located. Having met the amicable and frenetic 'Johnny' Zhuang, we were invited to his restaurant and later to a salsa dancing night. From hanging around Johnny's network it soon became clear that any straightforward idea of a Chinese community in Ghana was nonsensical, something confirmed by Ho's study (2008). In Ghana, being part of Johnny's network meant regular visits to his restaurant for business parties with karaoke and heavy drinking, with communications through the internet. But from there Dr Tan-Mullins met other businessmen. What became clear is that this was a newer Shanghaiese group who were quite distinct from an older Hong Kong group, some of whom had come shortly after independence to set up manufacturing plants in what was a 'model' colony that was predicted to blossom economically. In Angola, the internet played an equally if not more important role in the expansion of the Chinese community. Most of Dr Tan-Mullins' first contacts in Luanda were established via the internet and QQ chatline, which facilitated relatively easy access to the Chinese compared with Ghana. We discuss these 'virtual communities' in more detail in Chapter 4.

In terms of the scale of the firm, the private entrepreneurs generally had one or two small companies in the trade, service or light manufacturing sectors. This compared with the larger multinationals, such as Sinohydro, which were effectively enclaved and had no substantial relationships with the small firms. Workers stayed on site in these work camps and had little interaction with Ghanaians outside the work context. That said, we managed to track down the Chinese staff working on the bigger projects at the times and places where they interacted locally. So, we met engineers on Labadi Beach near Accra on a Saturday and drivers outside building sites. Crucially, Dr Tan-Mullins' Chinese heritage meant that these approaches were relatively casual and not obviously about research. In the second project, Dr Lampert started in Lagos where many of the trading firms were based. Larger firms, such as Huawei, have offices there and other firms have headquarters in Abuja, the Federal capital.

Negotiating difference and researcher effects Our main research method was autobiographical interviews with these entrepreneurs and employees, who generally saw Africa as a real economic opportunity. What we were not prepared for was the degree of cultural and racial difference expressed by some respondents, especially the older generation, which we discuss in Chapter 5. These strong senses of difference not only contradict the official discourse of 'South–South' harmony and collaboration, but more importantly presage different types of economic relationship with Africans. While the *guanxi* of the Chinese family firm may be somewhat mythologized, this lack of respect for and trust of 'Africans' shapes the nature of inter-firm relations. This sense of difference and a perceived threat was also used to explain why some Chinese socialized together though, as we noted earlier, this self-imposed segregation is far from hermetic.

So, while there was no innate sense of Chinese-ness or community there was a relational dynamic of immigrants banding together in contexts where they felt unwelcome.

Being a woman researching in these locales presented a unique set of challenges. In Angola, the Chinese migrants we met seemed more obliged to 'protect' Dr Tan-Mullins as a woman, especially in situations where it is considered 'dangerous' and she was perceived to be more vulnerable. There were occasions when Dr Tan-Mullins was stopped from going to certain places or meeting certain people as they were considered 'unsafe'. As a result, she had to shield some of her Chinese informants from her plans in order to avoid these unnecessary conflicts.

In terms of being Chinese, the language and cultural familiarity were the biggest advantages, as it made fieldwork and interviewing Chinese informants easier. This was particularly true in Angola, as the main language was Portuguese instead of English. Hence, it was always more relaxing for our respondents to converse in Mandarin/Cantonese. However, at times it worked against us. For example, some informants were unwilling to talk to Dr Tan-Mullins about more sensitive political issues, especially in Ghana during election time, fearing that she might know too much and put them in a difficult position.

Outline argument and structure

This chapter has established the importance of Chinese migration to Africa, but noted certain deficiencies in existing approaches to the subject. These concern disciplinary divides, a tendency to focus on economic drivers at the expense of a more rounded picture of these flows, and a focus on elite actors to the exclusion of more everyday relations between a diverse range of Chinese and African actors. We have proposed a framework based on Stephen Castles' work and argued for integrating political economy and culture more thoroughly. This means we focus on the globalization of China and Africa as well as how these global forces touch ground in Africa. Methodologically this called for a qualitative approach looking at the organization of Chinese migration, the perceptions of the actors involved and the relationships between them.

In order to appreciate the ways in which China has changed and how this affects outward migration, Chapter 2 examines the social and cultural history of Chinese migration. It is broadly a periodization, which shows the historical depth of ties between China and Africa. The purpose of this history is largely to show how some of the preceding flows of migrants left their traces on more contemporary migrations. In doing this we did not want to simply tell the story of elites and policy frameworks, though these are there, but to bring in the social history of these changes. Hence it is not simply a state-centred view of changing policies but about how people have lived, experienced and driven these changes. Most notable was how some of the older Chinese migrants we find in Africa today had clear memories of the hardships under Mao and how this conditioned both their motivations for coming to Africa and their relationships with both China and Africa.

The question still remains: why Africa as a destination for Chinese? Chapter 3 focuses on the more recent history of why Africa is important for China and what motivates migration and which actors are operating there. The starting point for this history is the 1990s reforms and the Going Out policy. Here we have disaggregated the range of actors (such as firms, officials, individuals) and their motives, which are more than simply economic gain. This latter point is important since we are keen to distance ourselves from readings of Chinese engagement with Africa as only an issue of resource and market access. Clearly, we cannot ignore such motives, but by seeing these as the only motives many accounts then paint a very 'thin' portrait of Chinese migrants, which lacks any humanity.

If the previous two chapters deal with major trends, albeit tempered by accounts of the individuals bound up in these events, then Chapter 4 unpacks the details of how these migrants operate socially and economically. The starting point for this is the firm and we use concepts from economic sociology to understand how these businesses operate and how they function as organizations in a different cultural context. It begins by looking at the debates about Chinese culture and capitalism that are heavily inspired by Weber. While useful for our analysis, such framings tend to focus on cultures and capitalisms in isolation and not the relationality of economic and social processes. So, we look at the ways in which family firms operate and the gender dynamics within them. We also look at the role of more formal ethnic and business associations, although these have only a limited role in coalescing Chinese communities in Africa, which remain fragmentary and fluid. All these practices are conditioned by the places where they take place.

Chapters 5 and 6 can be read as a pair insofar as the first of them deals with social tensions between some Chinese migrants and some Africans, and the latter with the more convivial aspects of these relationships. Chapter 5 focuses on the more adversarial relations around race, hierarchy and resistance and rather than look at Africans as the 'victims' in this encounter – as western critics of both the left and right tend to do – we look at the relationality and positionality of the actors involved which presents a much more dynamic and contradictory picture. At times we see quite clear hierarchical racial and class-based logics in operation, where the Chinese migrants do exploit local society, but at other times African actors exploit Chinese labour. Indeed, this focus on African agency in this relationship runs throughout the book and helps us move away from an image of an all-powerful Chinese presence.

Chapter 6 also focuses on relationships between Chinese and Africans, but this is much more convivial and hospitable. Too much reporting of Chinese migrants focuses on the tensions they release, as part of a wider attempt to demonize China's rise globally. As with the previous chapter, it focuses on the creative use of the relationship with Chinese actors for Africans. It mirrors many of the concerns of Chapter 5 and examines how Chinese and Africans are coming to know each other in quite subtle ways as the relationships endure. It looks at how competition within economic sectors elicits creative and sometimes mutually enriching exchanges. At the inter-personal level we find many cross-cultural friendships and an ease that feeds into the long-standing cosmopolitanism of African cities. Chapter 7 is the conclusion, which provides a summary and suggests some overarching theoretical and policy issues raised by our findings.

2 | CHINA'S OPENING UP: INTERNATIONAL-IZATION, LIBERALIZATION AND EMIGRATION

Introduction

With a few exceptions (e.g. Snow 1988; Bräutigam 1998; Li 2012; Mohan and Tan-Mullins 2009; and Monson 2009), the literature on Chinese migrants in Africa tends to take China's political and economic reforms of the 1980s as the starting point for discussion. In this chapter, we take a longer view when examining the relations between China and Africa to illustrate how key events in modern Chinese history have triggered the movement of people, goods and services beyond the borders of China. We outline the historical periodization of Chinese contact with Africa, from as early as the Han dynasty until the rise of Communist China, to demonstrate how Chinese policy and changing domestic circumstances prompted or prevented people from leaving China.

Such historical depth matters in terms of understanding the periodization of migration and its relationships to geopolitical forces. Although migration in general has largely been shaped by the demands of the capitalist world economy, such structural analyses can conceal important ways in which capitalism works through the exploitation of difference, particularly race and gender (Silvey 2004). It can also overlook the geopolitical drivers, which may be part of a desire to access markets but which may also be about political considerations that are relatively autonomous from capitalist imperatives. This chapter assesses the drivers of Chinese migration, the source regions for migrants and the patterns of settlement in Africa, both geographically and over time. Running through this broad-brush history are the perspectives of those who lived through the changes. We examine how men and women have experienced these changes, triggered by drivers such as historical events, domestic policy shifts, geopolitical manoeuvres, gender dynamics and economic incentives.

The next section examines how events, notably the Opium Wars and colonialization in the 1800s, contributed to early waves of Chinese migrants to the colonies of England, Germany and Spain in Africa. Following that there is a section analysing how conflicts, revolutions and closure in China due to the civil war in the 1930s–40s and the Cold War of the 1950s–80s brought about another flow of migrants to the newly independent states of the African continent. In this section, we examine the rise of Communist China and its impact on people's ability and willingness to move out of China. In addition, we assess how geopolitical rivalry during the Cold War affected the provision of foreign aid, which in turn brought Chinese workers to the African continent for the purposes of 'developmental cooperation'.

The last section assesses the recent phenomenon of Chinese migration into Africa from 1979, with China's opening up and liberalization programme. Deng Xiaoping's Open Door policy of 1978 marked a turning point in domestic policy from relative closure to an embracing of globalization. Here we assess a range of Chinese emigration and economic policies to get a sense of how the state viewed the need to make connections beyond its borders. Finally, the typologies and distribution of Chinese in the continent are discussed to tease out these changing typologies throughout the different periods.

Before embarking on this analysis of historical events and drivers of change, we need to address the debates about 'Overseas Chinese', which is a term that has been used loosely by many scholars. There are numerous Chinese terms equivalent to the English use of Overseas Chinese, ranging from Huaqiao (华侨) or Huayi (华裔) as Chinese citizens or ethnic Chinese residing overseas, and Haiwai Huaren (海外华人). The latter term denotes a highly problematic category as within this word also co-exist different forms and classes of migrants, mainly problematized by the sovereignty issues of Taiwan and Hong Kong (prior to 1997), and different clans marked by geographical, linguistic, cultural and political differences. In Africa, often speaking different languages, let alone identifying themselves as a coherent group, the Chinese have flexible identities and generate greater or lesser senses of community among themselves, depending on a range of factors (Wilhelm 2006; Hsu 2007; Ho 2008). In some cases, clans and associations organized along the lines of dialect groups further exacerbated the lack of interaction between these groups. In Madagascar, for example, from the nineteenth century, the migrants of Cantonese origin adopted political tactics to ward off any Hakka living in the same administrative area, such as by dominating the position of congregation heads, who represented the Chinese population living in the area and acted as a mediator between the local Chinese community and the Madagascan government (Live 2005).

Although these regional and cultural fissures play a significant role in contributing to the lack of collectiveness of the 'Chinese' migrants, we found, however, that economic competitiveness is a more important reason for lack of interaction and a sense of community, with the older established Chinese communities from Taiwan and Hong Kong resentful of the recent, seemingly avaricious arrivals from mainland China. As such, we found limits to social interaction between different Chinese sub-groups in our field sites.

China meets Africa: early contact and the 'coolie trade'

Although the evidence is inconclusive, the earliest contact between China and Africa can be traced back to the Han dynasty (206 BC to AD 220). Prior to AD 618 according to written accounts, albeit ambiguous, and archaeological evidence, goods from China and Africa reached each other through intermediaries such as the traders from the Middle East and North Africa. From 618 to 1368 (Tang, Song and Yuan dynasties), evidence can be found for direct and more frequent indirect contacts between China and Africa. For example, porcelains from the Song and Yuan dynasties have been discovered in Egypt, Sudan, Morocco, Ethiopia, Somalia, Kenya, Tanzania, Zimbabwe and Madagascar (Li 2012).

Between 1368 and 1450 (first half of the Ming dynasty), various emperors commissioned systematic expeditions by land and sea. As a result, contact between China and Africa, and China's understanding of Africa, were enhanced considerably (ibid.). However, during the late Ming period, domestic instability – such as the failed coup in 1461 and increasing Japanese pirate attacks on Chinese merchant ships – saw the introduction of the *Haijin* laws, which banned private maritime activity until their formal abolition in 1567 (Fairbank and Goldman 1992). Such isolation continued and became increasingly entrenched during the Qing dynasty (1644–1912) as a result of the negative experience of trading with the westerners and later a series of wars with the European colonial powers. This Chinese isolationist approach was most evident in the post-1949 period, when Mao Zedong discontinued diplomatic relations with many countries.

In terms of emigration policies, during the Ming dynasty (1368–1644), legislation opposing migrants moving out of China was influenced by the wider geopolitical events of the region. The *Haijin* laws were tightened due to an attempted uprising in Taiwan during the Qing dynasty (Shen 2006). Perspectives on Overseas Chinese were best reflected in the political discourse, which could be summarized as: 'no one was allowed to sail to another country and those who were caught will be put to death' (ibid.: 203). As a result, Overseas Chinese were considered traitors and unprotected, as best illustrated in the Red River 'incident' in Jakarta in 1740 where more than 10,000 Chinese perished after a rebellion against the Dutch. Emperor Qianlong (1735–96) showed no anger but complained: 'They disgracefully abandoned their ancestors to gain fortune in an alien country, so they would be abandoned and would receive no sympathy or support from the government' (ibid.).

In the early Qing period, due to the isolationist policy, official relations were replaced by private contacts and indirect trade, such as smuggling, replaced direct trade. Due to colonization of Africa and Asia, China's interaction with Africa was increasingly mediated by European powers. Indentured Chinese labourers became the primary agent in Sino-African relations (Li 2012) contracted and mediated by Europeans. For example, by the mid-seventeenth century as the European imperial powers took hold of more and more territory, they brought Chinese labour to Africa to work the ports and undertake menial tasks (Chang 1968). The Opium Wars (1839–42 and 1856–60) are generally considered to be the watershed whereby China was forced to open its door to the wider world. The Opium Wars were waged by Britain against China to enforce the opening up of Chinese ports to trade in opium. The first Opium War resulted in the concession of Hong Kong to Britain and the opening of the five treaty ports licensed for foreign trade, and the second Opium War forced China to sign a treaty to consent to more trading privileges for a number of European countries. The Europeans took advantage of the social and economic upheavals caused by the Opium War treaties and the Sino-Japanese War, and they enticed the Chinese as contract workers to South Africa. The Treaty of Peking in 1860 officially withdrew the Chinese ban on emigration (ibid.). From this point onwards, European countries began to have a strong influence on China's economic, political and social landscape.

It was during this period that we see the beginning of large-scale movements of Chinese overseas in the form of the 'coolie trade' (ibid.; Park 2006). The literal translation of 'coolies' (苦力) from Mandarin to English is 'hard-working labourers' and they were famed for their diligence and willingness to undertake any kind of work (Chang 2003; Tung 1974). As such, there was a rise in recruitment by the French and British for indentured labour. Subsequent domestic socio-political and economic troubles, such as the unrest surrounding the Sino-Japanese War of 1895, the Eight Nation Invasion in 1899 and the Russia–Japan war in north-eastern China in 1904, prompted many Chinese to escape the country and eke out a living overseas.

In 1904, after a series of negotiations with French and British ministers, the Qing dynasty government consented to a series of agreements for the easy transport and exit of Chinese contract workers out of China. As a result, a huge number of contract workers (coolies) were exported as 'willing migrants' to work in South African gold mines (Huynh 2008). Further demand for plantation labour and railway construction coupled with push factors in China, including land pressure and conflicts, saw France begin its recruitment of Chinese indentured labour to Madagascar, Mauritius and Réunion Island. Another example was the 491 Chinese and Indonesian labourers brought to Tanganyika by the German colonial administration to produce cash crops in the Usambara mountains towards the end of the nineteenth century (Karugia 2010).

In terms of numbers, approximately 70,000 Chinese contract

workers came to South Africa between 1901 and 1910 (Li 2012). Most of these labour contracts were highly regulated and workers were sent back after their contracts expired. The colonial authorities treated the Chinese as intermediaries who were neither 'black' nor 'white' and they were even introduced to show the apparently 'slothful' Africans how to work hard (Wilhelm 2006). The Chinese tendency towards hard work and financial prudence earned them the disparaging title of the 'Jews of the East', which some Chinese migrants re-appropriated as an argument for citizenship since they presented themselves as disciplined and law-abiding (McKeown 1999).

However, indentured labourers and Chinese coolies are over-represented as the paradigm of Chinese migration in the colonial period. Although not all coolies were indentured labourers, Chinese movement to Africa was restricted to small numbers of these labourers, convicts and slaves (Yap and Man 1998). Free Overseas Chinese in Africa were rare since the Chinese government, and the wider social discourse, regarded Overseas Chinese as traitors who had abandoned their country in collusion with the British colonizers. It was not until the 1870s that Chinese sojourners arrived as free immigrants, chasing rumours of gold and great wealth. These groups eventually became settlers, the ancestors of today's 'local' Chinese population (Park 2006: 203). There were also small, but enterprising groups of independent traders who serviced Chinese labour migrants and undertook small-scale export. From the late nineteenth century in South Africa, independent artisans and family trading firms constituted the oldest communities, known today as 'local' Chinese, who are distinctive from more recent arrivals (Wilhelm 2006; Park 2006). According to Park (2006: 208), these 'local' Chinese originated from the Guangdong area and arrived after 1870; through seven decades of experiences in South Africa, they forged a unique Chinese South African identity. In Madagascar, according to a French census of 1904, there were 452 independent Chinese migrants on the island (Zhang and Wang 2005). These Chinese remained in the host countries and in many cases the migrants became citizens, intermarrying with the local population, such that up to 60 per cent of the Chinese in Madagascar are ethnically mixed (ibid.).

Conflict, revolution and closure: the rise of Communist China

The preceding section outlined how the geopolitical and economic rivalries between the various colonial powers in the nineteenth and early twentieth centuries were important drivers of Chinese migration into Africa. However, changing domestic circumstances such as socio-political upheavals and economic challenges were equally important in encouraging the Chinese to move out of China. The influence of domestic conflicts continued with the fall of Qing dynasty and rise of Communist China, with Cold War rivalry triggering another flow of Chinese migrants into Africa, albeit under very different geopolitical and economic circumstances. At the same time, there was a limited emancipation of women under the communist system. One upshot of these changes in gender roles and relationships was that some women emerged from the domestic sphere into the public sphere through work and were able to migrate to Africa. The gender dynamics of Chinese migration to Africa has hardly been touched upon and is a theme running from here onwards in this book. This section will discuss the complex and intertwined drivers of Chinese migration into Africa by looking at the domestic conflicts and the creation of Communist China.

The revolutionary nationalist movement, the Kuomintang (Chinese Nationalist Party), was originally funded by Overseas Chinese and gathered momentum towards the end of the Qing dynasty. On 1 January 1912, the Republic of China was proclaimed and by 12 February of that year, the Qing emperor was forced to abdicate (Gray 2010). A period of chaos, political unrest and social upheaval ensued as a result of the power struggle between a number of military cliques, supporters of the Qing emperor and the Kuomintang (McCord 1993; Waldron 2003). However, in 1927 rivalry between the Kuomintang and the Communist Party of China led to a split in the troops, with the former consolidating its power base and establishing the new government in Nanjing in 1928. At the same time, the Communist Party of China began to exert influence in the eastern Jiangxi province with official war declared between the two forces in Shanghai in April 1927.

The late 1920s to around 1950 was a turbulent time in China. In addition to a bloody and prolonged civil war (1927–50), China was fighting the Japanese (the second Sino-Japanese War, 1937–45). The Chinese civil war was fought along the ideological lines of nationalism and democracy versus communism. The Communist Party of China advocated land reform and relied on peasants and workers for support; using guerrilla warfare tactics, it eventually triumphed over the nationalist forces. By the end of 1949, the Nationalist Party retreated to Taiwan and within a year approximately two million people including refugees and armed forces had followed the Kuomintang to Taiwan (Li 2001).

Due to their different ideological beliefs and the fear of being persecuted, a number of well-off industrialists from the mainland migrated to Hong Kong and then moved on to Africa and South East Asia. As the Kano-based daughter-in-law of a pioneering Hong Kong Chinese industrialist in Nigeria stated: 'The Communists were coming. We feared them very much. Being someone who had money and property, my father[-in-law] had to flee China. He went to Hong Kong first then later on came to Nigeria.'

This is by no means an isolated case. We found that a number of Chinese families arrived in Africa from the late 1940s and subsequently became pioneer industrialists there. For example, a Lagos-based Hong Kong-Chinese restaurant manager, whose father was another of the Hong Kong-Chinese industrial pioneers in Nigeria, recalled:

> In 1950s and '60s the Hong Kong business and Chinese business is not so good, especially after the People's Republic of China was established. All those rich people ran from Shanghai to Hong Kong. They brought a lot of money, technology, and equipment. So then they establish factory in Hong Kong but Hong Kong by that time it's not so boom and then the opportunity in Nigeria. So they invest money, come for Nigeria.

In 1941, there were 3,637 Chinese migrants on Madagascar (Zhang and Wang 2005), rising to 5,000 by 1950 (Pan 2005). In Zanzibar, the first batch of individual migrants came from Canton in the 1930s and found a niche, particularly in the food sector; they became an integral part of the local population, mirroring early Chinese migratory flows to other parts of the world (Hsu 2007). Initially, settlement was an urban phenomenon with the Chinese settling in primate cities or coastal ports (Chang 1968; Hsu 2007; Haugen and Carling 2005), but some soon dispersed into rural areas, many of them remote and poorly supplied with basic infrastructure. As such, South Africa, Madagascar, Mauritius and Réunion became the four main destinations of Overseas Chinese during that period. South Africa, in particular, continued to attract Chinese migrants from Taiwan and Hong Kong and hosts one of the most long-standing and established Chinese communities in Africa (Park 2006). This predominance of Taiwanese and Hong Kongers in these four African states was partly because under Mao Zedong (1949–76) the movement of mainland Chinese was greatly restricted. Not only were the mainland Chinese not able to emigrate but they could not move easily within mainland China. As a result, Chinese migrant families that have lived and worked in Africa since the 1950s tend to have originated from Taiwan and Hong Kong.

It has been noted in other studies, both historical and contemporary, that many Chinese migrants in Africa operate in relatively frugal ways, eschewing the lifestyle and trappings of successful business people (e.g. Haugen and Carling 2005). Again, some of this willingness and ability to endure relative discomfort can be traced back to experiences of the Maoist period and the hardships attendant on a rapid transition from less developed to developing country status. Prolonged separation during the civil war, the Cultural Revolution and the Great Leap Forward also helps to explain why the Chinese migrants we studied were willing to endure separation from family members in their move to Africa.

The culture of prolonged separation began during the civil war period, as many Chinese families were divided for several decades between mainland China and Taiwan and Hong Kong before they had an opportunity to be reunited. Under Mao, family life in China was fractured, with people being sent to labour camps, detention facilities, state farms and cadre schools during the Great Leap Forward. At this time, people who were critical of the government or were considered to be 'counter-revolutionary' were sent to labour camps where the inmates were subject to back-breaking labour and sometimes starvation

(Chang and Halliday 2005). Their living conditions were basic with no furniture or washing facilities. As sanitation was poor, diseases were rife (Williams and Wu 2004). This context of relatively recent hardship is important in the contemporary China–Africa story, because the older informants who lived through this period discussed their success in Africa in terms of their tolerance of prolonged separation from their families. Alongside their ability to work hard and endure long working hours, they also seemed to be more ready to take risks, given that they had already lost everything during the Cultural Revolution.

This hardship and frugality extended into the Cold War period. Here geopolitical strategy was played out in Africa with China challenging the major superpowers through its conspicuous targeting of aid (Snow 1988; 1995). Chinese aid was used to cement 'South–South' solidarity and provided visible evidence that China was not interested in playing power politics on the continent, while all the time doing precisely that (Taylor 2006a). The outcome of this was not only financial grant aid, but prestige construction projects (e.g. courts, state houses) and teams of technical advisers, especially in the areas of agriculture (Bräutigam 1998) and health (Hsu 2002). In terms of construction, two famous examples are the TAZARA Railway and the Friendship Textile Factory in Tanzania (Monson 2011). Between the 1960s and the beginning of the 1980s (with the exception of the Cultural Revolution), at least 150,000 Chinese technical assistants were dispatched to Africa (ECOWAS-SWAC/OECD 2006). Given the ideological climate these workers often went with a missionary zeal but little knowledge of the countries to which they were posted. Zhou Enlai encouraged them to live humble lives, again in conspicuous contrast to the supposedly indulgent western aid workers.

The current experiences of some of our older informants in Africa certainly corroborate the characterization of life during the Mao era. An example of this is a Lagos-based Chinese woman in her mid-fifties who manages a hotel and restaurant, having moved to Nigeria in the late 1980s. She recounted stories of great loss during the Cultural Revolution because her family was seen as 'capitalist'. The family lost its properties, land and a number of family members. Furthermore, she and the rest of the family were sent to different labour camps.

In the labour camp, she tilled land for about ten hours a day every day for very little money (approximately 18 RMB per month). She said this taught her how to 'eat bitterness'. She recalled how life in Nigeria in the late 1980s to early 1990s could not have been more of a contrast to her life during the Cultural Revolution. Business was lucrative, with around a 500 per cent mark-up on imported goods, and she felt she had nothing to lose having experienced the horrors of the Cultural Revolution as a young girl.

During the Maoist period, these political and social upheavals also played an important part in changing Chinese women's roles and wider gender relations. Prior to 1949, the practices of concubinage and child betrothal were common. Women took little or no part in public affairs and they were restricted entirely to the domestic sphere. Parents arranged marriages and encouraged patrilocal residence (whereby the couple establish their residence near or with the husband's family) which ensured that a woman had no claim over her own labour. When the Communist Party of China gained power in 1949, it adopted a number of legal, economic and political policies and programmes to actively redefine the roles of women. The aim was to place women in a position of equal status with men in both the public and domestic spheres. One example was the 1950 Marriage Law, which implemented marriage, divorce and inheritance rights for women. By placing 'marriage' (a previously private transaction) within the public purview, women gained more freedom, entitlements and legal protection (Bailey 2012).

Prior to the economic reform, the reinforcement of the Household Registration System (户口) had restricted the mobility of both women and men. Under the Household Registration System, each Chinese citizen was categorized as either a 'rural' or an 'urban' resident. A rural resident could only convert their status into 'urban' and be granted the freedom to move to urban areas by fulfilling stipulated criteria. Since the economic reforms, the restrictions on movement have been relaxed greatly, and many Chinese men and women have taken advantage of their newly found mobility to search for a better life. By the end of the 1990s, there were nearly 130 million rural labourers and migrants in urban areas (ibid.). The experiences of women rural migrants in China deserve further examination as they share a number of similarities with Chinese women migrants in Africa in terms of more agency, autonomy, independence and enjoying a more equal relationship with their husbands.

China's opening: liberalization and the 'new' Chinese migration

The economic challenges became prevalent after Mao Zedong's death in 1976. Domestic economic difficulties brought about by years of revolution, in addition to an inefficient commune system and an ineffective distribution system, prompted Deng Xiaoping, the then leader, to embark on the 'Reforms and Openness' (改革开放) programme in 1978. It was also partly attributed to the changing geopolitical situation, the rise of regional economies in East Asia, and the rapidly globalizing world where western firms were seeking to relocate production to cheaper and more 'flexible' sites. Based on Deng's famous slogan of 'It does not matter if it is a black cat or white cat, as long as the cat catches the mice, it is a good cat', it implied a move towards a managed capitalist system. These policy changes inevitably had a big role in influencing people's willingness and ability to migrate to the African continent. Indeed, as Mung (2008) indicates, the most important factor influencing more recent Chinese migration is the opening up of the People's Republic of China (PRC) and the liberalization of emigration controls that increased the willingness of Chinese to migrate overseas.

From the late 1970s under Deng Xiaoping's leadership, domestic policy and perceptions of Overseas Chinese started to shift. Many migrants in our research attributed the change in people's perception of and the motivations to move to Africa to Deng's policy. As the founder and owner of the Lagos China Town complex asserted:

Deng Xiaoping the then Premier had this policy of encouraging the bringing in of foreign investments into China and the exportation of Chinese investments and Chinese culture and encouraging the Chinese people to go out into the world to ensure that world international arena understand and know about China. (Interpreter's translation from Chinese)

Previously seen as traitors, these migrants were then perceived as agents of some sort of communist 'mission' and progressively as agents of modernization through economic ties. The establishment of the Overseas Chinese Affairs Commission in 1974 demonstrated the early intent of the Chinese state in 'actively seeking to retain transnational ties to the millions of Chinese citizens and ethnic Chinese spread across the globe' (Thuno 2001: 910). This shift is important to Overseas Chinese who were regarded more positively and accepted by the Chinese government; they were able to engage in tangible activities linking them to home in the form of remittances and charity (Young and Shih 2003; Zhu 2006). Park (2006: 203) notes that: 'Deeply held beliefs in the great China myth contributed to the Chinese state's success in maintaining a psychological and emotional hold over the Chinese diaspora.' According to Skinner (1976), it was precisely because those who left could be counted on to return that a person with aspirations to get ahead could expect support from members of their local community beyond the limits of family and lineage. In other words, the positive perception of these migrants and their ability to retain a 'bond' with the homeland enhanced the migratory flows of Chinese to Africa.

The PRC's strategy of actively appealing to and liaising with ethnic Chinese around the world can be attributed to economic pragmatism. As Thuno (2001: 928) notes: 'By emphasizing regional bonds and national sentiments, the PRC successfully solicited investments and donations for *qiaoxiang* areas where ethnic Chinese were free to express their cultural and social belonging.' Since the early 1980s, the PRC governments have been keen to attract the wealth of the Chinese diaspora (Young and Shih 2003) through laws and less direct appeals to the cultural affinities of migrants. This is a strategy found in other developing countries (Levitt and de la Dehesa 2003), but it has been especially successful in the case of China where as much as 65 per cent of China's foreign direct investment (FDI) had come from Overseas Chinese by 2011 (Chen 2012). On top of this, in 1985 there was a 'neutralization' of emigration legislation (Biao 2003), seeking to disentangle outward movement from geopolitical and ideological concerns. It is now much easier for Chinese business people, and tourists, to travel outside China. Having settled in Nigeria in the late 1970s, a Taiwanese guesthouse and restaurant manager in Kano observed: 'When I came to Nigeria that time hardly to see Chinese from mainland China. Hardly. Because that time China not yet open their doors. They not yet allow their people going out. Not like now.'

In the 1990s, as China's economy began to experience resource shortages and internal competition, the government built upon the inward FDI-seeking Open Door policies by developing the Going Out policy. The Going Out policy was implemented in 1999 and included the total or partial privatization of state-owned enterprises (SOEs) and a concerted internationalization strategy that has seen increased Chinese investment overseas (UN 2007). This policy, with clear benefits for the 180 approved SOEs such as preferential finance, tax concessions and political backing, provided incentives and financial support for these companies to 'go global' (Alden and Davies 2006). Many of these concessions were manifested in government-linked contracts through aid-funded projects in Africa, which further developed Africa as a major destination for both state-led projects and independent entrepreneurs.

While much of the impetus for the Going Out policy was market access for its SOEs, the other major driver was the need to secure raw materials for future growth. From the mid-1990s onwards, China became a net importer of oil and this saw an engagement with those countries and regions that produced oil and other strategic minerals, many of which were found in Africa. To facilitate this trade, one important mechanism was the Forum on China–Africa Cooperation, which aims to explore and implement effective methods of achieving beneficial China–Africa relations in various areas of activity. During the summits in 2000, 2003, 2006, 2009 and 2012, China's loans, aid and ways in which China will contribute to 'improving' Africans' livelihoods and the development of Africa were discussed. Against this need to import raw materials, the booming Chinese economy created a glut of cheap manufactures requiring markets. This has seen a wave of economic migration to Africa by major state-influenced construction teams and mining and oil workers, as well as private traders (Broadman 2007).

As a result, although there was an increased volume of migration flows to North America, Australasia and Europe from the beginning of the liberalization of Chinese emigration laws in 1985 (Skeldon 2011), other key sites of settlement in the 1990s and 2000s are mainly resource frontiers. In Africa this has meant regions such as the Copperbelt in Zambia (Trofimov 2007) or trade routes, such as that between Namibia and Angola (Dobler 2005). Some settlement has been as a result of additional policy decisions, such as in and around export processing zones in Mauritius (Lincoln 2006) and Taiwanese firms setting up in selected South African homelands in the 1980s (Pickles and Woods 1989; Hart 1996). There has also been a significant deregulation of labour recruitment and a growth in private labour contractors in populous provinces such as Sichuan, Hubei and Henan (Wong 2006). For example, in Lujiazhuang in Dingzhou city, Hebei province, 70 per cent of the village labour force works abroad and 90 per cent of those workers headed for Africa ten years ago. In 2011 the remittances from these approximately 2,000 international migrant workers from Lujiazhuang earned around 50 million RMB (Chinadaily.com.cn 11 June 2012). The combined effect of these movements, as we noted in the previous chapter, resulted in an estimated number of Chinese in Africa of around one million (Chinadaily.com. cn 11 June 2011).

At the same time as it needed to access resources, China's economic policies culminated in an increasingly competitive domestic business environment, especially with the accession into the World Trade Organization in 2001. With increasing business opportunities and rising living standards, more and more people were able to obtain financial support, either from local sponsors (such as relatives or banks) or international business partners to start new businesses. However, this economic growth has meant that competitiveness has been unsustainable in China and pushed entrepreneurs out of the country. As the long-established, Lagos-based Chinese hotel and restaurant manager quoted above contended: 'So another reason why there is an exodus of Chinese into Africa is that the Chinese market is saturated so they come out' (Interpreter's translation from Chinese).

This competition further extends to the African marketplace. An example from our fieldwork concerns the Ningboese, a regional group of Chinese, geographically located 100 kilometres south of Shanghai, who have a sizeable presence in Lagos. They speak a distinctive Ningboese dialect, are proud of their Ningboese cuisine and favour their own cultural group for marriages and business operations. However, their strong regional identity at home did not translate into close business links in Lagos due to competition between Ningboese businesses. We observed that most large SOEs benefit from the various support schemes and linkages set up by the Chinese government with their local African counterparts, while the small to medium-sized enterprises and individual entrepreneurs were mostly left to their own devices when it comes to business operations, opportunities and setting up in Africa.

This push of migrants out of China into Africa was also made possible by better information about doing business in different parts of Africa. There are now numerous websites set up by different arms of the Chinese government as well as private operators that offer platforms for disseminating information and connecting new arrivals at their destinations. An example is the 'qufeizhou.com' (http://bbs.qufeizhou.com 去非洲) which literally means 'go to Africa' and provides a substantial database of news and information about all fifty-five African countries. Many African cities also now have branches of the international banks in which the Chinese government is a substantial shareholder and they offer services to their Chinese customers. For example, in 2011 the Bank of China launched a Chinese Desk in Ghana in collaboration with the Ecobank of Ghana to facilitate the needs of local Chinese enterprises (Bank of China 2011). This banking arrangement was intended to ease the transfer of capital in and out of Africa, although local informants in Ghana and Nigeria complained that they often have to change the money into US dollars first before converting it to RMB to be sent back to China, making transfers complicated.

Conclusion

This chapter has sought to examine the drivers of Chinese migration to Africa. These have shifted from the Opium War treaties between Britain and China that saw the beginning of movements of Chinese overseas in the form of the 'coolie trade' in the 1800s, to migrants escaping the political upheavals in the 1940s, to the economic migrants of the post-Open Door policy period of the 1980s. The PRC's economic pragmatism of the 1980s led to the Chinese state re-engaging with the global processes of mobility of people, images and ideas, which influence the imagination of Chinese transnationals (Barabantseva 2005). As illustrated by Park (2006: 203), China maintained 'tremendous influence on overseas Chinese in South Africa and elsewhere in the world. Chinese, including those in South Africa, imagined that they belonged to a once great mythical China.' Accompanying these events and policy changes were personal circumstances such as women's relative emancipation and economic enhancement, which encouraged people to move.

While we have deliberately avoided a 'push and pull' logic, this chapter has been about how China's engagement with the world in general, and Africa in particular, has evolved over the past centuries. As illustrated earlier, sustaining and expanding people's livelihood has always been an important driver for migration (De Haan 1999). This could be 'forced' or 'voluntary', depending on how severe the resource, ecological and economic conditions in the sending country are (Van Hear et al. 2012). In addition, structural and institutional factors also created outward movements, which we saw in the form of Chinese fleeing to Taiwan and Hong Kong in the 1940s. These kinds of migration then could be classified as illegal, professional, student, refugee, family, marriage and so on (ibid.).

Structural forces have operated differently in different periods and, overlying this, the migrants have also been labelled differently given prevailing perceptions and academic trends. So, we have seen paradigmatic – but ultimately incomplete – histories which break time into distinct periods: the era of coolie labour, aid workers in the Cold War, and entrepreneurial migrants in the late twentieth and early twenty-first centuries. All such periodization flattens the diversity of migrants and we have tried to show through the limited numerical data that exist and some of our own respondents' testimony that there are important differences

TABLE 2.1 Typologies of Chinese migrants in Africa

Type of migrant	Motivation	Period	Events/drivers	Source in China	Destinations in Africa	Occupation
Indentured	Forced	1800–1906	Colonialism, Opium War	Coastal provinces of mainland	South Africa Madagascar Mauritius Réunion Island Tanzania	Miners Railway workers Farmers in plantations
Political/ economic	Forced	1911–79	Civil war Cultural Revolution	Mainland China (especially Shanghai, Canton) Taiwan Hong Kong	Zanzibar South Africa Madagascar Mauritius Réunion Island	Entrepreneurial businessmen Technology providers
Aid workers	Forced	1949–79	Geopolitical rivalries with United States and Soviet Union	Mainland China	29 African countries (1979) including Togo, Tanzania and Zambia	Healthcare, agronomists technicians, builders, engineers etc.

Economic/entrepreneur	Free	1940s–80s	Economic difficulties in Hong Kong	Hong Kong	Western Africa	Business persons
Economic/entrepreneur	Free	1970s–80s	Political 'outcast' solidarity	Taiwan	South Africa	Business entrepreneurs
Economic/entrepreneur/	Free	1979–current	Competition in China Attraction of Africa	Mainland China, Hong Kong, Taiwan, Macau	Africa island and continent	Individual, small, medium, large private enterprises, specializing in manufacturing, trade and services to produce niche market goods
Aid workers/temporary labour	State-led/impelled	1979–current	SOEs-led project Aid projects such as infrastructural and energy construction	Mainland China Hong Kong Taiwan, Macau	Africa island and continent	From low-skilled construction workers to middle and high-level management staff

Sources: Xinhua (2011); Kragelund (2010); Li (2012); Chang (1968); Huynh (2008); Yap and Man (1998); Park (2006); Pan (2005); Hsu (2007); Haugen and Carling (2005); Mung (2008); Thuno (2001).

in motivation, source regions, destinations, and social roles and relationships.

This diversity of drivers is important, because current movements are influenced by these previous waves of migration. This influence may be subtle at some times, and more direct at others. This chapter has demonstrated that flows of Chinese migrants to Africa have been influenced by domestic political, economic and social changes and wider geopolitical events, and constrained or promoted by personal circumstances. However, these factors are just part of the equation and the African responses to Overseas Chinese are equally, if not more, important for an understanding of different Chinese settlement patterns in Africa, which we discuss in later chapters of the book.

Table 2.1 (pp. 48–9) summarizes the changing typologies of migrants in different periods due to these different drivers. Unlike the past when migrants came from a specific region (coastal, colonies) and went to mainly island or coastal African countries, what is notable in recent times is that we are seeing a mass migration of Chinese from all provinces and regions from China to both island and continental Africa. The number has also increased tremendously, although precise numbers are questionable.

What we see in the most recent wave of Chinese migrants from late 1990s, who are the main focus of our book, is a movement of mainland Chinese, both as part of state-led projects as well as privately organized. In Africa, according to Mung (2008), although classic labour migration still plays a part, other types of migrants are increasing due to the social and regional composition of the Chinese migrants. Mung argues that the most prominent forms of migrants in Africa are now temporary labour, entrepreneurial and transitory migrants. In our fieldwork, the transitory migrants were less evident, partly because they are harder to find. That said, the issue of deportation of illegal Chinese migrants from Ghana became big news in both China and Ghana in late 2013 and may presage an era of more purposive policy to deal with such unlawful flows. Despite our lack of data on transitory and illegal migrants, many of our informants did cite an important reason for moving to Africa: the relative stringency of immigration policies in western countries. However, we found no intent to move to the West immediately through immigration loopholes in Africa. The question of African immigration laws raises important issues about the conditions in Africa that encourage or dissuade migration from China. The domestic and geopolitical factors discussed in this chapter cannot explain why Africa was selected as a destination by Chinese migrants. It is to the draw of Africa that we now turn.

3 | AFRICA AS OPPORTUNITY: CHINESE INTERESTS, MOTIVES AND ASPIRATIONS

Introduction

The dominant explanation for the Chinese presence in Africa is to access the continent's vast resources and emerging markets. In such accounts, aid is used as a form of 'soft power' to smooth entry into these markets that have hitherto been the preserve of western multinational companies. This materialist and realist explanation has much traction and tends to be tied to state actors (although in China the distinction between state and non-state is complex) in the shape of large state-owned enterprises (SOEs) (e.g. Sinohydro) and banks (e.g. ExIm). In terms of geopolitical discourse, this has seen a shift from ideological solidarity in the Cold War period, where African regimes were courted as part of an 'anti-imperialist' movement, to a more clear-cut and aggressive business footing in the recent past. This shift is reflected in our attitude survey, which showed that 96 per cent of Ghanaian respondents and 71 per cent of Nigerians were aware of a Chinese presence in their respective countries, although the Lagos figure was 92 per cent. In both countries around 70 per cent of respondents felt that the numbers of Chinese had gone up in the past five years.

However, other interests exist which are not the same as the Chinese state's although they are not totally detached from them either. In this chapter we address, but also move beyond, the state-centred accounts about why Chinese migrants come to Africa and present a more rounded and diverse picture based on multiple actors with different agendas. Through examining the interests of independent business migrants, we aim to identify the rationales for choosing Africa as a destination of emigration. These migrants work in a range of firms, from large private companies (such as Huawei) to 'suitcase multinationals' with one or two Chinese owners and/or management. In between we find sizeable private enterprises built by more established Chinese migrants in Africa, such as the groups of family-based firms developed by long-standing Hong Kong Chinese entrepreneurs in Ghana and Nigeria. Moreover, migration determinants and motivations are important factors in shaping the length of stay in the host country and daily interactions with the host communities (Mayda 2005). This chapter addresses the question: Why Africa and the recent migration waves to the continent? By evaluating why Africa is considered a viable and attractive destination from various perspectives, we provide a background for understanding migrants' behaviours in the host countries.

In the following section we examine the state-led geo-economic and geopolitical motives for engaging with Africa. Scouring for natural resources, new markets and investment opportunities, building strategic partnerships with Africa in the global arena (especially on the 'One-China' policy) and development cooperation were often cited as the main geo-economic and geopolitical drivers for increasing China–Africa interactions and their attendant flows of Chinese migrants to the continent. Although the state provided the main push in the 1990s to early 2000s, what is also important are the motives of small, medium and large private enterprises and individual migrants. In this chapter we will discuss the positive outlook of many of the continent's economies in terms of market and investment opportunities; the compatibility between the goods and services offered by Chinese enterprises and the purchasing power of the African consumers; and the better wage and job prospects available to some Chinese migrants in Africa. The chapter then moves beyond these narrow economic motives of market, investment and employment opportunities to address wider aspirations driving Chinese migration to Africa. In this part, we will explore motivations framed in terms of altruism and solidarity as well as a desire for self-development and, particularly for some female respondents, greater social freedom.

'China-in-Africa': state interests and geopolitical drivers

Existing explanations of the increasing Chinese presence in Africa have focused on state-led drivers, although this has begun to change in the past few years. These state-based geo-economic and geopolitical motives are refracted through official bilateral aid and developmental projects, ranging from access to natural resources and new markets, 'South–South' solidarity and building political alliances on the global stage (e.g. Davies et al. 2008; Huang 2007; Kragelund 2008; Lancaster 2007; Staehle 2007). Carmody (2011: 5) summarizes this argument in which Chinese involvement in Africa is explained by the 'geo-economic competition between different world economic powers to open up resource access for their companies, in addition to subsidiary moves such as getting access to African markets and seeking diplomatic support in the United Nations'. Our attitude survey showed that most Africans were more aware of the business opportunities the Chinese were pursuing than they were aware of aid and diplomatic reasons. However, a diploma-educated 53-year-old Ghanaian male working as a manager noted:

> I am very sure the relationship between government of Ghana and the Chinese government is motivating them to come. Formerly we didn't have these Chinese here much, only a few of them. But now that our government went there to look for aid and the rest, it has become a morale booster. It shows that the government of Ghana has friendly motives and so they will be very happy coming to Ghana and do business.

He clearly sees inter-state relations as crucial for the growing presence of Chinese in Ghana.

Alden's (2005) early framework for disaggregating the Chinese state's African interests still holds true. He identifies three considerations for increasing China–Africa relations as: (1) China's drive for resources, security, new markets and investment opportunities; (2) symbolic diplomacy and development cooperation; and (3) forging strategic partnerships. China's burgeoning domestic demand and export-oriented manufacturing sector required huge resources, such as oil, gas and minerals, to sustain their growth. At the same time, Africa was able to provide a new market for low-value consumer goods produced in China. In addition, China's image has been promoted in Africa through a series of high-profile infrastructure projects on the continent, while such partnerships were part of a wider geopolitical goal of countering American hegemony. Realizing the importance of the African bloc in terms of votes at the United Nations and other international platforms, African countries were seen as vital partners in China's global ambitions. As a result of these factors, Chinese engagement with Africa has gathered pace, especially from 2006 onwards.

Following Alden's three-fold schema, one of the major drivers of Chinese engagement with Africa has been the question of Taiwan. As we saw in the previous chapter, out-migration from China for much of the Cold War period was highly restricted, particularly after 1949, when the People's Republic of China (PRC) was formed and the Kuomintang withdrew to Taiwan to form the Republic of China (ROC). Taiwan is important for the Africa migration story for three reasons. First, Taiwan is one of the most significant parts of the 22 million strong Chinese diaspora, and many Taiwanese firms operate in Africa (Pickles and Woods 1989; Hart 1996). Second, political tensions between supporters of the PRC and ROC still exist among diaspora communities. Third, the PRC has pursued its 'One-China' policy since the formation of Taiwan and gives favourable aid terms to African countries that support its claims to Taiwan.

The formation of the PRC came at a time of a polarizing world order and while Africa was relatively unimportant in absolute terms, its sovereign states had some leverage in these grand geopolitical manoeuvres. For China, Africa has been important since the late 1950s, when Chinese diplomacy began to emerge, in the aftermath of the Korean War, from the shadow of the Soviet Union (Taylor 2009). Africa was a continent where the powers rallied for support and votes, especially in global platforms such as the United Nations Assembly where African countries were enlisted by China in support of its 'One-China' policy. As such, there are only four African countries which support Taiwan's claims as a sovereign country today: Swaziland, Burkina Faso, São Tomé and Principe and Gambia.

While diplomatic support between China and African states existed between 1949 and 1955, there was little movement of Chinese nationals to Africa as the Chinese Communist Party sought to safeguard the security of China and to assure the survival of the communist regime through stringent emigration regulations. The engagement with the African continent was evident bilaterally and at international platforms such as the Bandung Conference in 1955. At the ideological level, China sought to wrest the leadership of the international communist movement from the Soviet Union and so criticized both the United States and the USSR in its overtures to African leaders. During the decolonization process and post-independence period, China's position as a non-colonial power also facilitated its presence in the African continent (Larkin 1971) and is used today as evidence of its long-standing 'peaceful' intentions in Africa.

In the 1970s and 1980s, there was an increased number of migrants from Taiwan and Hong Kong, mainly to South Africa. In general, these migrants were either middle-income professionals or entrepreneurs. A 'political outcast solidarity' saw South Africa and Taiwan maintaining economic and political relations (Pickles and Woods 1989) when other states severed ties with the apartheid regime. Partly because of the international embargoes placed on South Africa, the country relaxed its migration policies to attract new migrants, an important group being highly skilled migrants from Taiwan. During the 1980s, some 300 to 400 Taiwanese industrialists set up in South Africa's peripheral regions. At the peak of these flows, there were between 30,000 and 40,000 Taiwanese living in South Africa (Wilhelm 2006). In 2000, the United States introduced the African Growth and Opportunity Act, a preferential trade quota and duty-free entry for sub-Saharan Africa's goods to help develop African economies. This had a significant impact in East and Southern Africa (Kaplinsky and Morris 2006) and was used by Taiwanese firms to re-import into the United States. Similarly, in Madagascar, the first Malagasy Republic (1960–72) maintained diplomatic relations with Taiwan instead of China, and saw a considerable number of Taiwanese migrants. However, in 1972 the second independence-era government severed relations with Taiwan and the numbers of Chinese migrants declined from 9,069 in 1967 to 4,039 in 1975 (Live 2005). In the 1980s, other geopolitical events, notably the collapse of the communist bloc in Eastern Europe and the Tiananmen Square incident, also prompted

China to strengthen its alliances with Africa (Raine 2009). After the Tiananmen Square incident in 1989, China came under extreme pressure from its erstwhile economic partners in the West (Taylor 1998) and found in Africa a supportive constituency (Kopinski et al. 2012).

Although these geopolitical drivers played a part in China's foreign policy towards Africa, it is geo-economic pragmatism that has come to dominate Chinese engagement with Africa. In the last chapter we briefly chronicled China's rapid growth following the reforms of the 1970s and how in the mid-1990s resource squeezes saw the country turning to external sources for raw materials. China's massive domestic growth in the late 1990s created a huge demand for resources and Africa presented a viable and untapped supply of resources *and* a market for its cheap exports (Downs 2007; Taylor 2006b).

For the Chinese state, Africa is attractive in terms of providing the types of commodities China demands. Africa is believed to possess a significant proportion of global mineral reserves: 30 per cent of bauxite, 60 per cent of manganese, 75 per cent of phosphates, 85 per cent of platinum, 80 per cent of chrome, 60 per cent of cobalt, 30 per cent of titanium, 75 per cent of diamonds and nearly 40 per cent of gold (France Diplomatie 2008). The continent also has substantial oil and gas reserves. According to the 2011 BP Statistical Energy Survey, at the end of 2010 Africa had proven oil reserves of 132.1 billion barrels or 9.5 per cent of the world's reserves. In 2010, the region produced an average of 10.098 million barrels of crude oil per day or 12.2 per cent of the world total (BP 2011), with new finds coming on stream in the Gulf of Guinea and East Africa. According to the same BP survey, at the end of 2010 Africa had proven natural gas reserves of 14.7 trillion cubic metres (7.9 per cent of the world total) while natural gas production for 2010 was 209 billion cubic metres (6.5 per cent of the world total). These strategic resources have seen inward investment and trade with certain African countries increase, pushing their growth rates into double figures in some cases. China has been central to this new 'scramble' for African resources and the country depends on Africa for 80 per cent of its cobalt imports and 40 per cent of its manganese imports (Foster et al. 2009) while Angola became the main African exporter of oil to China from 2008 with around 16 per cent of China's oil originating there. Indeed, the abundance of natural resources in Africa has 'led Beijing to seek long-term deals with African governments that ensure continued access to all raw materials and sources of energy' (Taylor 2009: 19).

Securing energy resources became an important dimension of Chinese interests in the African continent, but not the only motive. As recognized by the Vice Premier Zhu Rongji as early as 2000: 'Africa, on the one hand, boasts talented and hardworking people, abundant natural resources, great market and development potential. China, on the other hand, has got considerable economic strength, a promising market and a wealth of commodities, managerial expertise and production technologies suitable to African countries' (Rongji 2000).

China has successfully engaged Africa in terms of access to the local markets, either through trade, bilateral aid or foreign direct investment. For example, Chinese trade with Africa stood at US$817 million in 1977 just before the reforms (Servant 2005) and reached a record high of US$166.1 billion in 2011, with China becoming Africa's largest trading partner (SAFPI 2012). On the investment front, China's overseas foreign direct investment stock in Africa increased from less than US$400 million in 2000 to over US$14 billion in 2011 (ibid.). In 2008, revenue from China's contracted and engineering projects in Africa rose to US$28.1 billion (CAITEC 2010).

As mentioned in the last chapter, some 180 SOEs were designated by the state to 'go global'. Estimates are that there are 2,000 Chinese companies investing in Africa, and with this a recurrence of temporary labour migrants (UPI 2013). A major growth sector for Chinese SOEs and private firms is in engineering and construction, which are generally labour-intensive activities. Driven by state-led policies, these SOEs represent a substantial amount of investment in Africa and require relatively large amounts of semi-skilled and skilled labour. The United Nations estimates that Chinese financing (including financial assistance and aid) has gone mostly to roads, railways (US$4 billion) and hydropower generation (US$3.3 billion) (UN 2012). The Chinese now have major infrastructure projects in thirty-five African countries, most funded by the ExIm (export–import) bank at 'marginally concessional' rates, and in many cases funded through natural resource deals and bilateral aid projects, such as the African Union Conference Center and office complex in Addis Ababa, Ethiopia.

In addition to their economic and geopolitical significance, SOEs, state-backed projects and bilateral cooperation programmes are identified by Chinese respondents in Ghana and Nigeria as key drivers of the first wave of new Chinese migration to Africa in the 1980s. As the Accra-based managing director of the Ghana branch of a Chinese state-owned construction company observed:

> After '80s, 1980s [...] the mainland China starts [to] come to the West Africa, or come to Africa. Like Ghana here, I think the first people come around the government [...] like some project, donation, the projects all between the mainland China government and the Ghana government, to have the agreement between the two governments to send some groups to come, like our company.

Furthermore, while it is not the most important driver, we found that migration associated with SOEs and government cooperation initiatives can have a direct link to the expansion of the Chinese entrepreneurial presence in Africa, with some individuals employed in these state-led engagements staying on to establish businesses of their own. For example, a respondent active in the Chinese community in Nigeria reported that the long-established Taiwanese owners of a supermarket in Lagos first came as agricultural experts sent by the Taiwanese government, while a Chinese doctor running a private clinic in Tema recalled that he originally arrived in Ghana in 1985 on a government health exchange programme. Similarly, a respondent in Tema came to Ghana in 1991 with a state-owned construction company and stayed on once his contract expired to establish a building supplies company. For this respondent and the doctor in Tema, a key motivation for remaining in Ghana was a concern about the difficulty of re-establishing a career back in China. However, for a Lagos-based respondent who established a travel agency in 2007 after resigning from the state-owned airline that had sent him to Nigeria only a year earlier, the main reason for branching out on his own was to take advantage of the 'opportunity' he saw in the country.

Africa as frontier: economic opportunities at the edge of globalization

While much attention has rightly focused on the Chinese state and the encouragement of its SOEs and large private corporations, Ho (2008) argues that there are entrepreneurs who operate independently of Chinese state agendas even though the misguided notion of 'China Inc.' suggests the contrary. Much less attention has been given to the independent entrepreneurs who are also targeting African markets, often without any state backing. There has also been little research on small and medium-sized enterprises (SMEs) and large private companies based in China that are establishing branches and outlets on the continent.

Our attitude survey showed that many Africans were aware of these motives. In a follow-up interview with a 24-year-old, degree-educated Ghanaian woman working as an administrator in Accra, we were told:

> The Chinese in Ghana, well most of their activities as far as I am concerned, are centred on business opportunities and they are exploring business opportunities in the country. The majority that I know of are executing contracts – roads, building contracts – and the minority have smaller businesses like the restaurants, a few shops here and there.

As noted earlier, this focus on 'business' and 'the economy' was much more prevalent in responses than diplomatic and geopolitical motivations. It is interesting that when asked how they knew a particular person was Chinese our survey respondents tended to say appearance or language. In Ghana this was 59 per cent and in Nigeria 47 per cent. Yet in the follow-up interviews with a sample who claimed to know Chinese personally, on three occasions there was confusion about nationality. In one interview a Nigerian respondent referred to those working in 'LG', another talked about 'Hyundai' and a Ghanaian respondent mentioned 'STX'. All three companies are South Korean, so there is awareness of 'Asian' businesses and people who appear to be Chinese, but such misconceptions speak of a conflation of peoples. That said, the point being made in all three cases was that these firms do well out of Africa so from an African perspective it matters little whether they are Chinese or Korean.

For independent Chinese entrepreneurs and private firms it is Africa's positive economic outlook, its market size and position as a frontier of globalization that are key drivers. Africa witnessed renewed economic growth as early as the 2000s (Carmody 2011: 67) and has 'experienced an average growth rate of more than 5 percent over the past decade', a rate that has been only temporarily interrupted by the global economic downturn (World Bank 2013: v). Even with the global economic slowdown, Africa was home to four of the top ten fastest-growing economies in the world in 2008. With the recovery of North African economies and sustained improvement in other regions, growth across the continent is expected to accelerate to 4.8 per cent in 2013 (African Economic Outlook 2013). Africa then represents a sizeable market demanding affordable goods (Carmody 2011) and has been lauded by global business and management consultant firms such as McKinsey (McKinsey Global Institute 2012) and Ernst and Young (2012) as the next investment destination. However, this growth is highly uneven across the continent and within countries. For example, the gap between the 'African lions', such as South Africa, Algeria, Libya, Angola and Botswana, with GDP per capita of more than US$5,000, and other African states such as Rwanda, Uganda and Ethiopia is as much as tenfold (McKinsey Global Institute 2010).

In terms of how Chinese firms responded to this growth, Gu (2009) identifies five primary reasons for Chinese investment in Africa: (1) access to local markets; (2) intense competition in domestic markets; (3) transfer abroad of excessive domestic production capability; (4) entry into new foreign markets via exports from host; and (5) taking advantage of African regional or international trade agreements. These factors help explain the growing presence of Chinese SMEs in Africa that are responding to the new economic opportunities, largely independently of inter-state deals. That said, while African growth began to pick up in the new millennium, it is the Asia-induced commodity boom of the past decade that is generating most demand for the goods and services provided by Chinese SMEs in Africa. In this sense there are recursive connections between the state-to-state deals, commodity demand and the actions of private Chinese firms.

As some of Africa's economies look up, the Chinese are also in search of new markets for large-scale projects such as infrastructure, telecommunications and financial services (Raine 2009). Africa's period of lagging development means that there is a huge demand for infrastructure and investment in human capital. In countries such Angola and DRC, where post-civil war national reconstruction became a main driver for economic growth, the Chinese moved in by providing huge loans for infrastructural projects such as roads, power plants and telecommunication (Corkin 2013). For example, Huawei and ZTE, both privately owned but largely state-influenced enterprises specializing in telecommunications, have enhanced the internet systems in Africa by providing code division multiple access (CDMA) portable modems that tap into the telecommunication networks to access the internet. As we have noted, a number of scholars (e.g. Naim 2007; Chidaushe 2007; Phillips 2006; Manji and Marks 2007) were concerned that the Chinese might be 'unfairly' developing their foothold in the African oil, infrastructure and telecommunications sectors through soft aid and preferential lending. However, according to Moyo (2009: 111), 'bartering infrastructure for energy reserves is well-understood by the Chinese and Africans alike. It's a trade-off, and there are no illusions as to who does what, to whom and why.' It is this transparent business footing that has gained the Chinese much approval in Africa, in contrast to what some see as the duplicitous actions of long-standing western interests. But as we shall see, this open pursuit of profit has also raised public concerns in Africa over competition in certain sectors.

Africa also offers a good training ground and a springboard for Chinese private companies with wider global ambitions. Such companies can, for example, seek joint ventures with western companies already operating in Africa to gain experience, facilitate technology transfer and speed their development towards international competitiveness (Raine 2009). There is also some limited evidence of acquisitions with, for example, a Chinese mining company acquiring an Australian mining firm operating in Africa for its technology, securing a global supply of resources, increasing market share and achieving economies of scale in production (Huang and Wilkes 2011).

One means that the Chinese state has used to facilitate inward investment to Africa by Chinese firms is through Special Economic Zones (SEZs). Much of this logic was based on China's own experience whereby dedicated enclaves were created to provide special incentives and labour regimes, to enhance the competitiveness of relatively young firms and co-locate them with other firms within the value chain (Arnold 2012). In 2006, five such zones were proposed for sub-Saharan Africa in the Forum on China–Africa Cooperation and their development was tied to domestic pressures in China to augment the incipient internationalization of Chinese firms. As a Chinese manager at the Lekki Free Trade Zone in Lagos contended:

> [B]ecause of the skill problem of Chinese enterprises, you cannot see so many Chinese enterprises locating in developed countries. Maybe in developed countries [...] the only thing which Chinese enterprises can do is to do the merger and acquisition. [...] But in underdeveloped country, like in African countries, then what we can do is to build our own factories because we are more skilful and we are more experienced and more developed than these enterprises in Africa.

The SEZs help China's labour-intensive, less competitive and 'mature' industries, such as textiles, leather goods and building materials, to move offshore in order to reduce labour and transport costs (Bräutigam and Tang 2011). They may also enable horizontal integration of Chinese supply chains with SEZ-based firms, supplying key inputs to projects run by the larger SOEs. Indeed, a prime mover in the Chinese consortium involved in the Lekki project explained:

> I have been working in Nigeria for several years, it's about five, six years back, I was working in [an SOE] to do the construction work and we found we face a lot of challenges. Almost all the materials we are using must be imported, machinery must be imported, spare parts is not available so I think it is necessary for ourselves to build some factory or workshops to manufacture some materials [locally].

Such zones are also largely constructed by Chinese developers who have a direct link to the interested clients in China (ibid.). In the case of Lekki, it is a joint venture between China-Africa Lekki Investment Ltd made up of four Chinese state investors and two Nigerian partners (Lagos State Government, Lekki Worldwide Investment Ltd). Incentives such as discounts on the rent and special 'Chinese-only' zones within these zones were also proposed to attract Chinese firms, although respondents involved in the Lekki project emphasize that the zone is very much open to international investors of any nationality.

For many Chinese manufacturing enterprises, there is a need to identify new markets for their lower-end consumer goods as production has outgrown domestic demand. A Chinese entrepreneur in Lagos who imports production machinery from China and who is also an executive of one of the two main Chinese associations based in the city argued that the European and North American markets are difficult to enter and have limited demand for the relatively cheap, low-technology goods many Chinese firms produce. As a result, he contends, the attempt to 'push' goods abroad has had to target less-developed markets in Africa, South America and South East Asia.

In this context, Chinese respondents in Nigeria often reported that it is the sheer size and relative underdevelopment of the country's consumer market that makes it a particularly attractive destination for Chinese companies and entrepreneurs. For example, the Chinese manager working on the Lekki project mentioned above asserted:

> Nigeria is definitely a big market but the consuming ability
> for Nigerian people is still low. For Chinese products, they are
> cheap to some extent, it's cheap, so let me say maybe for Chinese
> product it's easy to suffice Nigerian people to consume the
> Chinese products.

Noting that Nigeria is the most populous country in Africa and has a 'very big' market, a Chinese trader in the Lagos China Town concurred:

> [T]he Chinese goods are much more acceptable in this market

here [...] in [a] developing country's market, because if you take them to the developed countries [...] the quality may be lower than what you have in those countries. But then it is similar or a bit higher than what you have in developing countries. (Interpreter's translation from Chinese)

Indeed, many of our African respondents indicated that the more affordable prices of Chinese manufactured goods make it possible for more Africans to purchase 'luxury items' such as fashionable shoes or handbags. While relatively few respondents (9 per cent in Ghana and 20 per cent in Nigeria) actually shopped in Chinese-owned shops, 37 per cent of Ghanaian and 48 per cent of Nigerian respondents claimed to have bought Chinese goods from any sort of shop in the last month. The main categories of goods purchased were clothes (20 per cent in Ghana, 15 per cent in Nigeria) and electronic goods (48 per cent in Ghana, 39 per cent in Nigeria). Their reasons for purchasing Chinese goods were cheapness (around 55 per cent across both cases) and, to a lesser extent, quality (around 13 per cent in each case). With the price of Chinese goods matching the purchasing abilities of many Africans, there has been a surge in demand for such goods across the continent. As a 32-year-old Nigerian teacher based in Lagos explained:

They have really enhance our way of living because now people buy things at a cheaper rate. They have made the cost of goods to be so low because in recent years before their products came out they were selling phone around 30 to 40 something thousand naira but now when you go to the market you see a China phone going for 6 to 7 thousand naira and they are of good products.

However, it is misleading to suggest that all African consumers want is the very cheapest goods. Africa also presents a sizeable middle-to-high-price quality market for Chinese manufacturers and entrepreneurs. Our fieldwork has shown that some Chinese enterprises not only target the mass market through provision of low-to-middle-price products, but also provide niche, up-market services and products. For example, we found Chinese businesses providing exclusive entertainment and restaurant facilities for African elites and Chinese expatriates working in the country. As a 24-year-old Nigerian graduate noted in our attitude survey:

> I get to know them [the Chinese] during my service year in Zamfara state, they have Chinese restaurant there and occasionally when we go there for chopping [eating] we meet them one on one because they like welcoming customers their self.

One of our favourite Chinese restaurants in Accra, Ghana, mainly caters to middle-class Africans and Chinese expatriates living in the country. Its exclusivity is guaranteed by its price range and location, being near the embassy area. In Luanda, Angola, a simple meal for ten people in the famous Chinese Dragon restaurant (with private dining and karaoke rooms) will cost approximately US$1,500.

In terms of servicing these markets, we see a range of strategies. In some cases China-based companies establish distribution outlets in Africa, but we also see Chinese entrepreneurs establishing firms in Africa to import a range of goods. In both cases, there is sometimes a transition to manufacturing or assembling goods in Africa itself. This is often related to a desire to be closer to the market, which saves the often high costs of importation and makes it easier to respond to local demand, but it can also be a response to African policy and regulations, such as the import bans imposed on a range of consumer goods by Nigeria in the early-to-mid 2000s. However, and as we examine in more detail later in the book, there are debates over whether these lower-priced goods are actually improving the living standards of the Africans, or driving out domestic producers.

However, it was clear that market size is not the sole consideration determining which African state to invest in. Chinese respondents in Ghana often claimed that while it represents a much smaller market than Nigeria, it has a more stable political situation. For example, a long-established Hong Kong Chinese manufacturer based in Accra emphasized that Ghana is a good place to do business because it is peaceful while Nigeria, where his brother is based, is 'messed up' and 'scare[s]' people. Similarly, a Chinese shop manager in Accra remarked: 'Nigeria is not so free as Ghana, maybe there is a problem of violence, or unstable, political instability. In Ghana it's relatively peaceful. I was told that throughout, during three decades, no political violence.' Furthermore, while there were widespread complaints about corrupt local officials in Ghana as well as Nigeria, the Ghana Investment Promotion Centre attracted some notable praise for encouraging and supporting foreign investment. For example, one of the most successful Chinese entrepreneurs in Accra believes that the agency is run by 'very good' people who want to 'help from the heart', not because they want money.

For Chinese migrants who come to Africa to take up jobs with Chinese companies, a key motivation is often the higher wages they are offered compared with working in China. In addition, employees of medium to large companies have many of their subsistence needs, such as food and accommodation, provided by their employers. According to some respondents who were employed by SOEs in Ghana, the only expenditure they have is to purchase international calling cards to phone China regularly. In some cases in Angola, especially with the bigger private enterprises like the China International Fund and SOEs such as the China International Trust and Investment Corporation, there are even landlines at work and in the accommodation with direct dialling facilities to China, to ensure that middle and senior management can contact their families regularly. In these ways, company employees have plenty of opportunity to save, especially as their augmented salaries are generally paid directly into their Chinese bank accounts.

So far we have discussed the geopolitical and economic motives for coming to Africa, which have tended to dominate existing explanations of Chinese engagements with the continent. But, not surprisingly, there are other factors at play, most notably personal development and a desire to see more of the world beyond China and acquire global experience and competencies.

Broadening horizons: self-development and the desire for global experience

In contrast to a discourse of 'the Chinese' as self-seeking or imperialistic, our fieldwork revealed more personal and intangible reasons for going to Africa. These included such things as extending one's horizons beyond China, developing global experience, and notions of altruism and solidarity. In terms of tangible skills, we found migrants wanting to acquire a European language, most usually English, and to augment their international business skills in order to improve their prospects for a career in international business, whether in other countries or in China itself. As such, numerous respondents, especially those in their twenties and thirties, expressed a strong intention to live beyond the borders of China, to experience a new country and to develop their own career paths as the main motives for their move to Africa.

These international experiences and improved language skills are deemed positive for upward mobility within and between companies, especially in the very competitive Chinese context. Related to this is a desire to develop hands-on experience in international business. This is especially important for young graduates who take jobs with Chinese companies operating in Africa and who sometimes go on to establish enterprises of their own. The most common reason was to improve skills in other international languages, especially English, which makes Anglophone Africa particularly attractive. For example, a university graduate in his late twenties who is employed as a restaurant manager in Tema wanted to 'polish' his English by coming to work in an Anglophone country so that he would have better prospects in the highly competitive job market in China. Similarly, in outlining his reasons for taking a job in Ghana, the Accra-based Chinese shop manager noted above, who is also a university graduate in his late twenties, remarked:

> First, Ghana is English speaking [...] Because English is the first of global language, more widely used than any other language in the world, so if you study English and go into business that require English then you have more opportunities. [...] So English is the first reason that we came to Ghana.

Furthermore, he added that his desire to develop his English-language skills is not only linked to improving his job prospects but is also central to his educational aspirations:

I want to study English to improve for my science studies, because in most Chinese universities, the textbooks will be written in English and you are supposed to write your thesis in English [...] Even if you want to test for post graduate [...] higher degree then you needed to pass English examination which is difficult for many people.

French was also mentioned as a desirable language by a few respondents. We met two respondents in China and one in Ghana who had recently taken up French lessons in order to pursue opportunities in Côte d'Ivoire.

Some respondents would ideally like to have gained their global experience in 'the West' but were unable to secure the necessary visas. In such circumstances, Africa became the second best option. For example, a Chinese student at a university in Ghana explained that the UK was her preferred study destination but the plan was dropped due to visa restrictions:

At first, I want to go to England to study but something wrong with my visa, so the embassy of British refused me. Because my father has business here for long time so and my uncle also live in Ghana and they suggest me to go to Ghana for study and they said that the education in Ghana is good, maybe better than China.

Moreover, the cost of living and studying in the West was seen as too high when compared with Africa. This illustrates how respondents often recognized that it is Africa that currently offers some of the most accessible opportunities for enhancing their global experience and education.

The desire to improve skills is related to personal social mobility and business success, but there are broader, more cosmopolitan motives that include a desire to see the world and learn about other places (see also Bourdarias 2010). Acquiring such experience is often highly valued in and of itself, and is seen as an important element of self-development. For example, a young Chinese employee working in a Chinese furniture company in Accra remarked, 'We dream to go around the world and see many different things and many different culture, different people', while the Accra-based Chinese shop manager mentioned previously contended:

> It's difficult to find a job [in China] that is interesting. Because if you find a job in China you can get almost the same pay in China, but as for young people like us, we want to find something interesting, exhilarating. [...T]o broaden your eyes and to see more about the world and to improve your understanding of the world.

We also found some respondents who expressed a particular interest in spending time in, and learning about, Africa as it is seen as a continent that is poorly understood and often misrepresented in China. These generally younger migrants came with a desire to 'debunk' the myths and stereotypes framing Africa as little more than a poverty-stricken and diseased continent. A case in point is a Tema-based Chinese factory manager in his late twenties who stated:

> Some Chinese people don't know much about Africa, the one thing they have learn from Africa is what they have been seeing on TV. It is unreal, not real, not realistic, so I also want to come to the real Africa and to see how the Africa really is.

Some older respondents framed their migration in terms of the historical relationship and affinity between Chinese and Africans and a sense of duty to cooperate in the continent's development. For example, a Chinese manufacturer also based in Tema but in her mid-fifties explained that when her husband completed his contract working in Ghana with a state-owned construction company, they considered what they could do to 'help the people' and decided to settle in Ghana because in her younger teens she 'heard what Mao Zedong said, he said that we should go to Africa and liberate Africa'. She took great satisfaction in reporting that through the small factory they established in Tema, they have been able to provide training and employment to locals, contribute tax to the government, and increase the 'friendship' between Ghana and China.

This illustrates how those respondents who frame their migration in terms of altruism and solidarity tend to do so in ways that mirror the official Chinese rhetoric of China–Africa development cooperation, in terms of mutual assistance and sincere partnership. Similarly, a Chinese executive involved in a state-backed project in Nigeria argued that as the intervention was unlikely to make any money in the foreseeable future, it was probably supported by the Chinese government as a way of 'helping' Africa.

In addition to the altruistic rationale for choosing Africa as a destination for migration, Africa offers a very different attraction specifically to some female respondents. Although similar economic rationales (such as market size/business contacts and career opportunities) do play an important role for our female respondents deciding to move to Africa, for some of them Africa was chosen because it offers a space and place to be independent and free from many of the constraints of contemporary female roles in China. In the next chapter we will explore gender relations in Chinese family businesses in Africa, but we have already seen that some female migrants took advantage of the increased ease to leave China. Those who had experienced the Great Leap Forward and the Cultural Revolution cherished the opportunity to go abroad and have an independent business. A number of informants explained that they were deprived of formal education and skills training in the 1960s and 1970s. As such, as a female informant in her early sixties said, women feel that 'doing business' is the only viable option open to them because it does not require any qualifications. A trader in the Lagos China Town who owns a ceramics shop and is in her mid-fifties said:

> I don't have much education so it was impossible to find a job when I was younger. Women of my age in China would be near retirement and feeling useless. Doing business is Nigeria is good. Have a shop here keeps me busy and I can work until I die... I feel young!

Hence, as soon as China was 'open' the older migrants saw the opportunities in Africa as traders, moving to Africa as early as the 1980s.

Younger migrants (in their twenties and thirties) see going to Africa as providing them with an opportunity to gain independence and adventure. A female migrant in her late twenties living in Kano demonstrates this well. After graduating from college, she found employment 300 miles from home. When she heard from an acquaintance that there were jobs to be had in Nigeria, she found herself a sponsor and an administrative job there. She travelled to Nigeria to work in one of the free trade zones without her parents' knowledge. Her mother only found out she was in Africa by chance but her father remains ignorant of her true whereabouts. When asked why she decided to leave China and why she was unwilling to inform her parents of her decision, she said: 'I want to be independent and to have an adventure. Working somewhere in China is not far enough whereas Africa is. I don't want my parents to know because I am a single child and they would not agree to let me go.'

During our research, we also came across a number of divorced women and single women who are over 30. Both categories of women would experience social pressure to some degree in China whereas Africa afforded them more freedom. One informant who owns a successful furniture business in Lagos and is in her mid-thirties said:

> If I was in China, my mother would nag me every day to get married. But I am in Africa and have my own business, I can do what I like without anyone telling me what to do. I don't like to go home because I cannot bear her nagging and everyone asking when I will get married.

Another informant also living in Lagos who manages a karaoke bar-cum-brothel said: 'If I do the same work in China, does not matter where I am my family will get to hear it. But doing what I do in Africa, no one at home will get to hear it.' We return to women migrants and questions of their 'independence' in the next chapter.

Conclusion

Geopolitical and economic factors are clearly key drivers of Chinese migration to Africa. However, there are also other important factors at play, most notably a desire to broaden one's horizons and gain global experience. In this way, Africa has not only become a continent of strategic and economic opportunity for Chinese state, corporate and independent actors but also a land through which desires for global knowledge and experience can be pursued. Acquiring such experience clearly has economic benefits in terms of career and business progression, but can also be seen as part of a quest for personal development in and of itself. This could, in turn, be part of a wider desire to engage with the world and develop cosmopolitan dispositions and competencies – a desire for global citizenship in the midst of China's international resurgence. Underpinning much of these movements are family and transnational networks that have played an important role in Chinese migration patterns to Africa, which will be the focus of our next chapter.

4 | CHINESE SOCIO-ECONOMIC LIFE IN AFRICA: NETWORKS AND REALITIES

Introduction

So far we have discussed the changes within China that have, over the years, precipitated movements out of the country in general and to Africa in particular. We also looked at the reasons why Africa became so crucial to the outward migration of Chinese from the mainland, Taiwan and Hong Kong. This necessarily broad-brush analysis obscures the organization of these flows and so in this chapter we examine in more detail the ways in which Chinese migrants are organized.

In looking at the realities of Chinese migrants in Africa we pick up on those debates from Chapter 1 about transnational Chinese socio-economic life that emphasize the importance of ethnic networks and community organization, particularly in explaining apparent Chinese business success. Such thinking is also evident in some of the recent work on the expansion of the Chinese presence in Africa (Gadzala 2009). By emphasizing ethnicity, these explanations tend to downplay how Chinese social and economic networks are shaped by class dynamics and also come to engage and incorporate non-Chinese actors. This chapter shows that while family and ethnic networks are undoubtedly important, Chinese socio-economic life is less cohesive and more locally embedded than is often assumed. Furthermore, the apparent assumption of business success also appears to be misplaced, with notable evidence of business struggles and failures.

The first part of the chapter outlines the ways in which Chinese businesses are structured around ethnicity and gender and connect both to their 'host' economies and global processes of accumulation. The second part outlines the nature of intra-ethnic social relations and the extent to which a Chinese 'community' can be said to exist.

The third part analyses the difficulties and dilemmas that Chinese businesses often encounter in Africa.

Chinese business organization in Africa: from ethnic networks to local embeddedness

Since research started on transnational Chinese businesses, a significant line of argument has developed seeking to explain the economic success of 'Chinese capitalism' in East and South East Asia (Kahn 1979; Berger 1987; MacFarquhar 1980; Crawford 2000). These studies posit Confucian values – such as strong family structures and ethnic networks – as underpinning the success of Chinese firms. It is argued that through such relationships Chinese firms are able to pool resources and share business intelligence. An early example of such thinking showed how subcontracting networks were created by Hong Kong Chinese in mainland China, in turn giving them a comparative advantage over non-Chinese firms (Crawford 2000). Studies focusing on Chinese family businesses have highlighted the importance of a patriarch who delegates key activities and positions to male members of his family. The patriarch's judgement is considered to be absolute and he has moral authority that encourages ties of mutual obligation. The same logic implies that Chinese family businesses are reluctant to admit professional outsiders into the senior management and, because the owners are also managers, there is a high degree of flexibility (Weidenbaum 1996). Furthermore, Bourdieu's concept of 'social capital' (1986) was extended to explain how Chinese businesses operate and benefit from networks and cooperation (Kuah-Pearce 2004). Notably, the idea of 'the strength of weak ties' (Granovetter 1985) was used to explain how kinship-based networks facilitated economic exchange without resorting to more contractual relations. Our research both supports and questions such observations, and we explore this by focusing on how and to what extent Chinese businesses in Africa utilize family labour and ethnic networks in getting established and expanding.

In Africa, the four pioneer states (South Africa, Mauritius, Madagascar and Réunion) which experienced earlier waves of Chinese immigration have seen higher social and economic integration between the Chinese and the local communities, either socially or politically. The higher level of integration was partly due to the Chinese emigration policy during that time, which was less welcoming to returnees as they were perceived to be 'traitors'. As Park (2008: 224) explains, the results of the civil war saw China adopt an isolationist approach and with 'China's doors effectively closed, Chinese South Africans found themselves "stuck" in South Africa'. As such, the tendency for these Chinese migrants to stay on and see the host country as 'home' was much higher. Further, with the inception of more lenient immigration policies in the 1980s, particularly for entrepreneurial Chinese from Taiwan and Hong Kong, there was a gradual increase in the number of Chinese granted permanent residence in South Africa (Harris and Pieke 1998). This was also demonstrated in Mauritius, where almost 30,000 Chinese migrants have taken up Mauritian citizenship. However, this trend towards political and social integration was not extended beyond these four major recipient states.

As we noted in Chapter 2, a number of Hong Kong Chinese business entrepreneurs (who had originated from Shanghai) began to arrive in Ghana and Nigeria from the late 1940s in the wake of the Chinese civil war. They tended to establish manufacturing enterprises, initially in enamelware and textiles, some of which have not only survived but also grown and diversified to become important players in the industrial and service sectors of both countries. The longevity of these firms has generally been built on inter-generational business succession and high-level managerial positions tend to be occupied by the sons of the founders or other close, often male, relatives such as sons-in-law and nephews.

For example, the Kano-based daughter-in-law of a pioneering Hong Kong Chinese industrialist in Nigeria described how her brother-in-law inherited and expanded the business and continues to make use of family labour in key positions:

My brother-in-law helped [my parents-in-law] a lot... he can speak he can write [English] and he also is hard working [...] he is the one who is building the business for our family. He has more than twenty factories in Nigeria [...] we have head office. [His] daughter,

daughter-in-law and the son-in-law [are] in Hong Kong office, head office and the son is with him in Nigeria running every factory.

However, we see the Confucian values that are often assumed to characterize Chinese capitalism being eroded with time in some instances. For example, succession tends to be more problematic when it comes to the third generation, where many have been educated and have citizenship in the West. They are not always as interested in manufacturing and living in Africa as their fathers, grandfathers or uncles were; their parents sometimes recognize this and put less pressure on them to join the family business. Others are left to choose their own professions and decide where to live. As a result, professional managers are increasingly employed to help run these businesses.

In keeping with much of the literature on transnational Chinese business, we found that family labour and capital are important not only to sizeable conglomerates but also to smaller, independent trading companies. These businesses tend to be thoroughly transnational, with family members recruited not only to manage businesses in Africa but also to source stock in China (see also Dobler 2009). As a female trader in the Lagos China Town explained: 'In China my daughter is there, so she just goes to lots of markets in China, a lot of the factories in China and sees what is good and then she sends to me. So I don't have any shipper, I don't have any supplier there, it's just my daughter.'

For those who prefer to employ family labour, the main motives appear to be the greater trust placed in family members. As the young manager of the Kano-based Nigerian wholesale outlet of his family's textile company explained:

[I]t is better you send your own relations here. Because for here, for example, we do many, many things, arrange your warehouse, sell the goods, transfer the money, there is no official receipt. Nobody would have it. [...] the price you putting in market any price they [employees who are not related] [...] call you say this price can sell [...] actually they are selling high price instead the price they told you.

A number of entrepreneurs of small to medium businesses express a desire to build a business legacy that will provide for future generations. A Lagos- and Kano-based Taiwanese manufacturer who first established a business in Nigeria twenty-two years ago explained the reason behind starting his latest enterprise in the country: 'one of my [business] partners he got two children at the moment they are 26, 27 years old [...] [they will] come Nigeria to start their business to start their life [...] that is why we try to concrete [...] foundation for them for development'. Speaking of his own succession, he said: 'my niece is already here and we keep telling them [the niece and the children of his business partner] we give them two years. After two years hand over to them.' However, as with conglomerates, succession can be equally problematic to these businesses. Some of the owners are willing to sell the business or hire professional managers when they retire because they realize that their offspring may have different aspirations.

In understanding Chinese business organization beyond family networks, a number of commentators emphasize the role of *guanxi*. *Guanxi* covers the relationships of privilege and is formed among status equals such as classmates, workmates, people with the same surname, or from the same locality in China (Nonini and Ong 1997). Given its emphasis on trust and social networks, *guanxi* is often equated with social capital (Bourdieu 1986). However, although Chinese capitalism can be seen to have distinct 'cultural' features, it has to be situated within processes of flexible accumulation that are inherent to global capitalism (Greenhalgh 1994; Dirlik 1997).

In the context of the Chinese migrants in Africa whom we interviewed, *guanxi* can be used to source goods, technology, labour and capital from China, which in return creates competitive advantage (see also Laribee 2008). As a Chinese entrepreneur based in the Lagos China Town remarked:

For people like us in China if you want a loan from the bank, it is very difficult unless you use your property. Only those big companies, government, owned by government, they can loan from bank anyhow. But people like us, you have to use your own

money. Like this door business, it's not my own one. We are [...]
four Chinese, we join together. I asked my friend and people who
I know, we joined together to do this one.

Illustrating how friendship connections and personal recommendations are often important for recruiting non-family labour, the
Chinese manager of a manufacturing company in Lagos reported that
a 'classmate' who knew the owner from school introduced him to
the company's Chinese owner. Many informants also used *guanxi* to
facilitate their migration. For example, a female informant managed
to find work in Lagos working in a karaoke bar via a friend who had
been working at the same job for a few years after she encountered
financial difficulty at home. Similarly, a male manager working for
a Chinese furniture company in Kano recalled a discussion he had
before he decided to take up the post:

> Actually, I did not know much about Nigeria, when I first came
> I was in Lagos but then I have a friend in Kano. We were class-
> mates. [...] I only asked him one question [...] what about security?
> He said 'ah, but Kano is more secure than Lagos'. So I was willing
> to move to Kano to work.

Despite this use of *guanxi* to source non-family labour, our
study indicates that there is a widespread 'professionalization' of
recruitment from China through internet job sites and employment
agencies, particularly of managers, sales representatives, technical
staff, translators and chefs (see also Park 2009). Such forms of recruitment have increased following liberalization. Many graduates
working in Ghana and Nigeria but employed by companies based in
China tend to find work by going through a competitive process of
shortlisting and interview in China. For example, a recent Chinese
graduate who works for an Accra-based Chinese firm importing fishing nets to Ghana said: 'I just sent my résumé to the company, you
can find in the internet [...] so everything is good. We just signed
the contract and came to Ghana here.' Explaining how he was recruited to be the Ghana sales representative of a China-based shoe
manufacturing company, another Accra-based informant said: '[The]

employment agency in China will identify what types of job you require, that you want and then you can apply. The boss will look at my CV and ask a couple of questions and if the boss is satisfied, then you are employed.'

As we noted, much of the discussion of Chinese migration to Africa is gender blind, insofar as it tends to focus on migrants as if they were all men. Moreover, the notion of Confucian capitalism assumes a male-headed family firm, where male relatives are given privileged positions. Ong (2002) argues that the academic discourse of Confucianism and *guanxi* have been used to gloss over the hier-archical and authoritarian relationships within the family firms that perpetuate inequalities. Greenhalgh (1994) argues that in order to compete successfully, the Taiwanese family firms in her study exploit the unpaid or low-paid family labour of women and young people. As such, she argues, the idea of this as a distinctly Confucian model is largely an invented tradition used to mask these exploitative prac-tices in a post-Fordist, flexible global economy. When women help out with businesses, they do so out of family duty and they are discouraged from moving into more challenging positions within the firm or from pursuing an independent career. In short, Chinese family firms are seen to be hierarchical and perpetuate inequalities of gender and generation.

Earlier we also discussed how social change in China resulted in the enhanced mobility of women, albeit within tight social con-straints. As a result, some women migrants see Africa as a place and space to gain independence and pursue adventure. During our research, we came to know many women migrants who chose to live and work in Africa. Some were employed to work in Africa and they tended to work in jobs that are traditionally more associ-ated with women (e.g. sales representatives, administrative staff, teachers, translators, waitresses and prostitutes). However, we also found women migrants' businesses that were not exclusively confined to the sectors associated with women but that were more diverse, including office equipment, restaurants and immigration advice.

We can gain a sense of women's instrumentality in these business formations and migration decisions from a Kano-based Taiwanese restaurant and guesthouse manager speaking about her mother-in-law, who was one of the first generation of Hong Kong Chinese migrants to Nigeria and who is now in her eighties, having retired to Hong Kong. She said:

> One time my mother-in-law she told me say why we came to
> Nigeria actually – my father-in-law he don't want to come
> to Nigeria, it's she who force him to come to Nigeria [...] my
> father-in-law still think consider, consider, he can't make up
> his mind and my mother-in-law say go, go you should try. My
> father-in-law say I don't think I can stay there because I don't
> speak English. Even Chinese he cannot read Chinese because they
> never go to the school. But my mother-in-law encouraging him,
> encouraging him. So finally he come with friends.

The informant's mother-in-law joined him shortly afterwards. The parents-in-law later established one of the largest Chinese industrial groups in Nigeria. The informant herself plays the leading role in the operation of the Chinese restaurant-cum-guesthouse that her parents-in-law passed on to her and her husband. Speaking of how the establishment is managed, she said: 'You see like this restaurant I can handle no even without my husband [...] If there is a problem I know how to run it.' A further example of a relatively equal gender relationship in a husband–wife business partnership is illustrated by a Chinese woman who is the lead manager of a number of retail outlets in the Lagos China Town. She is the eldest of four siblings and she and her husband take turns to be in Lagos, looking after the shops. When her husband is in China, he is in charge of sourcing, arranging customs clearance and shipping. When she is in China, she does the same.

Some male informants also suggested that there was relative equality of genders within some Chinese family business organizations in Africa. When asked about the division of labour within the family business, a small business owner based in Dar es Salaam said:

> [G]enerally I am in charge of meeting with clients and discussing
> business arrangements and my wife is in charge of the operation

of the factory. We have about twenty Tanzanian workers on the shop floor. The business is doing well because she manages the staff well and our operation is very smooth.

While we are not suggesting that all women are equally empowered relative to their husbands, these examples indicate that in some family businesses the idea of absolute patriarchy does not apply.

The migration story of one of our younger male informants echoes this. His wife studied in Europe and upon graduation was recruited by a European-owned company operating in Kano. Before our informant joined his wife, he worked in a commercial bank in China and looked after their child. Six years ago, after four years of the wife's posting, he and the child joined his wife in Nigeria. His wife has continued to work for the same company. Since his arrival, he has opened a successful restaurant and bakery in Kano.

Some of our women migrants were either the sole proprietors of their businesses or co-owned businesses with other Chinese or local business partners. They tended to be divorced or single women over 30. When asked about their experience of living and working in Africa, they often spoke of their freedom. For example, a Chinese woman in her early fifties who manages a shoe shop in central Accra contended:

> I am alone here by myself; I have no family, no husband or kids with me. If you have a family it is more difficult to travel abroad. Living abroad you are bound to be concerned about the family. Before when I wanted a child, I got married, then I had a divorce, I refused to remarry; since then I am very free citizen, highly independent. (Interpreter's translation from Chinese)

The experiences of these migrants show that 'Africa' seems to provide a refuge for women who do not conform to social norms in China.

Part of the Confucian capitalism argument relates to the formation of embedded 'ethnic economies'. Embeddedness has been used to analyse ethnic businesses, which often secure labour, contracts and inputs from members of the same ethnic or racial group (Granovetter 1985; 1995; Zukin and DiMaggio 1990). For newly arrived immigrants, 'participation in a preexisting ethnic economy can have positive economic consequences, including a greater opportunity for self-employment' (Portes and Jensen 1987: 768). Eventually, such ethnic communities can function as a 'market for culturally defined goods, a pool of reliable low-wage labour, and a potential source of start-up capital' (Portes and Sensenbrenner 1993: 1329). Most analysis in this vein has occurred in contexts of migration to developed economies, but clearly such theories support the commonly perceived organization of Chinese businesses in Africa.

We found some development of an 'ethnic economy' in which businesses provide goods and services to other Chinese companies and individuals in Africa. For example, some Chinese supermarkets, beauty parlours and restaurants in Lagos and Tema have predominantly Chinese clienteles. Small Chinese farming enterprises are known to supply vegetables to Chinese customers and some Chinese restaurants in Dar es Salaam, Lagos and Tema, and a Chinese telecommunications company in Nigeria uses a Hong Kong Chinese supplier for generators as well as some Chinese construction contractors. Some businesses, such as hotels, restaurants, barbers, travel agencies, health clinics and immigration advisory services, place adverts in the regional Chinese newspaper *West Africa United Business Weekly* which suggests a target market of fellow Chinese.

Although there is some evidence of utilizing wider ethnic networks to find work and advance their businesses in Africa, our informants sometimes emphasized that the decision to source inputs from China and indeed other parts of the world or locally is a commercial one. For example, a long-established Kano-based Hong Kong Chinese manufacturer asserted of his raw materials:

> [T]he one that can be locally available of course we prefer to take it locally, but again this is all commercial decision [...] I would say for majority of the business people whether Nigerian or Chinese or whoever, patriotism does not really come in. America is driving many Japanese cars because the Japanese car is good for the individual family. But if you try to impose patriotism, you ask them to patronize the America car, it's difficult.

Similarly, the Chinese manager of a curtain shop in Accra explained that sometimes the shop sources accessories (e.g. curtain rails and fancy rope) from Ghanaian traders when the stock runs low as it is difficult to ship small quantities of accessories in a container at short notice. In this case they purchase Chinese products from Ghanaians because doing so is cheaper. Therefore, the 'Confucian' theories of Chinese transnational capitalism might not explain fully the economic activities of Chinese migrants in Africa. In practice, we see complex and multi-layered value chains involved in delivering products to consumers (Chang et al. 2013). Since the opening up of the late 1970s, China has placed itself as a low-wage node in global value chains that ultimately deliver products to western markets. But Africa is also an emerging market for Chinese manufactures which are well suited to the relatively less affluent African consumer.

This demand coming from Africa is met by many independent Chinese businesses in Africa which import and sell to local consumers on a wholesale or retail basis. A Chinese entrepreneur based in the Lagos China Town articulated this well:

> [L]ike this suit, when I came to Nigeria in 2002, I didn't see many people, only some people working in a bank wearing suits. You can see everyone [...] if you went to church 90 per cent men they are wearing suits. They cannot buy suits from America because it too cost. They cannot buy. Even they can buy from India, but it costs.

Even enterprises that might at first be assumed to prioritize the Chinese population often focus on African customers. Notably, the number of Chinese restaurants in Accra and Lagos has expanded in recent years primarily to serve the growing demand of African middle classes and elites for Chinese food. For example, the proprietor of a Chinese restaurant in Accra estimated that 90 per cent of her clientele are Ghanaians and the manager of a Chinese restaurant in Lagos explained:

> Nigerian they are rich. Some of them are rich but they do not have a place to spend money, no entertainment place, so they like

to have party, like a birthday where they will spend their money. They spend one million, two million no problem.

Similarly, Chinese medicine clinics and wholesalers also tend to primarily target the African market.

Perhaps the most important way in which many Chinese enterprises have extended beyond ethnic networks and become locally embedded is through their recruitment of African employees. Contrary to the dominant assertion that Chinese companies operating in Africa tend to rely on labour imported from China, in most of the eighty-five Chinese enterprises we studied in Ghana and Nigeria, a substantial proportion, and often the majority, of the workforce was African. This was seen at a range of scales, from the independent Chinese traders in markets in Lagos and Accra who generally employ at least a couple of local assistants all the way through to the largest Hong Kong Chinese-owned industrial groups that employ thousands of African workers (Bourdarias 2010; Carling and Haugen 2008; Giese and Thiel 2012; Kernen 2010; Lee 2009; Hairong and Sautman 2010). Employing Africans is central to the business strategies of most of the Chinese companies we engaged with; this has important implications not only for how the Chinese presence is perceived but also for its role in local development.

Our research shows that Chinese business organization in Africa exhibits some of the assumed Confucian values posited by earlier literatures on Chinese migrant entrepreneurship. There was evidence of peer networks being used for finance and recruitment, but equally more arm's length and meritocratic means were being used to recruit staff. Moreover, we found cases where women's roles were not the subordinate and dutiful ones posited in the literature and wives enjoyed parity with husbands in their businesses. Likewise, as Dobler (2009) found among Chinese migrants in Namibia, the practice of ethnic economic networks does not seem to be as prevalent as is often assumed and it was more a case of decision-making based on logics of profit and loss.

Ethnic affinity and its limits: Chinese community organization and social life in Africa

In this section, we will further develop the ideas of ethnic embeddedness by looking at the wider social relations of Chinese migrants, particularly the more formalized organizations that enable group formation. While ethnic embeddedness is based on relations between people who are assumed to share the same culture, in reality cultures are not homogeneous. Furthermore, transnational migrants operate in multiple 'overseas' localities in which different social, economic and political histories unfold (Castles 2012; Tsing 2004). Hence, while 'embeddedness' suggests some spatially and historically essential characteristics, in practice as migrants disperse to multiple locations their social and cultural organization becomes shaped by those localities.

In order to examine the social and community life of Chinese migrants in Africa, we will first discuss their associational life. There are two umbrella Chinese business associations, often referred to as Chambers of Commerce, in both Lagos and Accra. These are more formalized modes of cooperation. Some of the chambers facilitate business networks as well as the relationship between the Chinese business community and both the Chinese embassy and the 'host' state. For example, one of the Chambers of Commerce in Ghana has a membership of companies and individuals, approximately sixty of whom are executive members who meet once a year. The membership of the other Chamber of Commerce in Ghana consists predominantly of state companies. While not representing formal organizations, some informants identify particular individuals as local Chinese 'leaders' who are conversant with the customs and the laws of the host country and from whom they can seek help if they encounter difficulties. In addition to representing the business interests of their members and facilitating network building, Chambers of Commerce also arrange social events for their members.

In terms of migrants' social life, our data indicate that long-established Chinese migrants, particularly of Hong Kong origin, often establish long-standing friendship networks. For example, a second-generation Hong Kong Chinese couple in Kano established a private club principally for their Hong Kong Chinese colleagues and friends. They have owned the business for thirty years. It was originally run by a number of partners (one partner was the wife's father) but after the partners retired or left Kano, the couple bought the remaining partners out and reinvented the club as a Chinese restaurant open to the public. Speaking about the closeness of the expatriate community in Kano in the 1970s, of which many of the Hong Kong Chinese were active members, the husband said:

> That time in Kano many, many Europeans are here, because it was a small community so everybody kind of knowing each other so every week we were invited for party. A very social type you know. And each party have a lot of people fifty, hundred. It's very actually very interesting and because a close community so you know you can make friends which many of them still last up to today. [...] I think socially people quite enjoying it. And at that time [...] the economy was good, security accordingly good. So at that time not much to complain.

The couple still hold a Chinese New Year celebration at their restaurant in Kano even though most of their Chinese friends have left, inviting Chinese residents of the city to join them for a banquet and karaoke.

Similarly, another second-generation Hong Kong Chinese migrant based in Nigeria echoes the same convivial spirit when he recounts the country's Hong Kong community:

> [O]ur Chinese Hong Kong we are very cooperate, you know, we are a family. So you want to buy something I can help you, you want to borrow this I'll help you. There's community [...] The Hong Kong network is more informal like everyone knows everyone... friends and family kind of connection.

Looking at more recent migrants, such conviviality is also found where co-workers not only work together but also live together. Co-workers of some of the enterprises we came to know live in the same compound, which makes socializing easy. The most common social activities are playing mah-jong, visiting beaches, playing sport, salsa dancing, cooking with friends, eating in restaurants and visiting the casino or karaoke bar. However, leisure time is restricted to weekends or parts of the weekend. The following response is typical. When asked what his and his Chinese colleagues' social life is like in Africa, a Chinese craftsman working for a Lagos-based furniture factory said:

> Most of times we are always working, if we go out at all it's just to the market to get one or two things from the market, that's all [...] when [we] have time on Sunday [we] clean up, wash [our] clothes [...] watch television, [we] just rest in the dormitory. (Interpreter's translation from Chinese)

Indeed, a number of informants noted that since they have access to Chinese cable channels, they now relax by watching TV programmes produced in China.

In terms of socializing more publicly, restaurants and karaoke bars are places where Chinese migrants tend to congregate in order to relax as well as conduct businesses. Many establishments are multi-functional with some restaurants incorporating karaoke bars that are open to Chinese customers for parties. Some karaoke bars in Dar es Salaam and Lagos we know provide sexual services in addition to food and drink. Casinos are very popular and although they do not offer sexual services directly, some of them serve as a contact point for Chinese prostitutes and their clients as confirmed by our informants in Dar es Salaam and Lagos.

Some Chinese migrants also visit the Lagos Confucius Institute, which is principally for Nigerians to learn aspects of Chinese culture. Confucius institutes are being established in major cities in Africa and are non-profit organizations seeking to promote the teaching of Chinese language and culture. The institutes offer lessons in Mandarin, Kung Fu, Chinese cooking, origami, Chinese opera, poetry and Chinese calligraphy. The Confucius institute places young volunteers who are newly graduated from universities in China and who are generally discouraged to leave the campus.

Sunday worship and other Christian gatherings are also opportunities for some of the Chinese migrants to meet and socialize. For example, a number of our Lagos informants attend the same Alpha course together, which allows people who are not familiar with Christianity to explore its meaning. The informants involved in the Alpha course meet weekly to have dinner and discuss their religious beliefs for their course work. They also go to church together on Sunday. A Ghana-based Chinese woman said that all her Chinese friends were made locally via her church. In addition to worshipping together, the informant and her Christian friends also celebrate Chinese festivals and national holidays together outside the church.

In parallel with these face-to-face networks we also found a lot of virtual networking among Chinese migrants, or would-be migrants from China. Yang (2003) and Ding (2007) looked at the potential of information and communications technology (ICT) for creating new associational forms. Shen (2009) explored the construction and perceptions of Africa among the users of the electronic forums in Mandarin. We build on these studies by looking at the social role that ICT plays in Chinese migrants' life in Africa.

When asked how he communicates with his family at home, a Chinese manager at the Kano branch of a Chinese furniture company responded: '[W]e contact our family by phone, by internet. A little [bit of] miss[ing home] of course for sure, but no problem.' The most popular software is Skype and QQ, which contains news in Mandarin and a facility for setting up email accounts and forums.

There are also numerous websites containing news about and adverts for jobs in Africa as well as online forums for people who are interested in learning about Africa or are about to migrate to Africa. Here they can share views and insights and find answers to their questions about Africa from migrants who travel widely in Africa or who have been living in the continent. When asked how much he knew about Ghana, the manager of a Chinese machinery import business in Accra said: 'I just checked from the internet before I come, a few information I think and I also add some friends who was in Ghana at the time to my QQ. The Chinese QQ. So I ask them some questions about Ghana before I come.'

Often migrants, especially young people, become virtual friends with someone who is already in their destination country. Once arrived, the virtual friends meet and consolidate their friendship. A

Lagos-based male informant in his early thirties recounted how he formed an online friendship prior to his departure for Lagos:

> I met Jo before I left China. I just wanted to meet someone who was already living in Lagos. So I decided to post a message in a forum and she answered my posting [...] we started to become friends that way [...] when I arrived Lagos, she and her husband were extremely helpful and kind to me [...] like my own brother and sister really [...] that is why I call her 'big-sister'. I often meet with her and her family and we spend time together [...] I am very pleased to have met her really.

In addition to making new friends, some informants also advertise their businesses in Africa via websites. For example, an informant who provides immigration advice and translation services for the Chinese who live or wish to live in Nigeria advertises in this way.

These convivial social networks sometimes form the basis for informal cooperation, such as exchange of information or goods or assistance in times of difficulty. When asked if he had received help from anyone when he first arrived, a Kano-based Chinese restaurateur and construction company owner said:

> I have one Chinese [who helped me when I arrived], he is from Hong Kong ... he stay Nigeria almost forty years – he helped me find first job. [H]e own factory in Port Harcourt also in Lagos, he every month go to Port Harcourt one times. He say tomorrow I go Port Harcourt you follow me that is why I follow him to Port Harcourt, he know the Chinese restaurant owner, it is his friend that is why I working there. He helped me. Even now I always say thank you.

Some commentators note that Chinese entrepreneurs, particularly traders, in a number of African localities are facing serious competition and declining profits (Carling and Haugen 2008). As a result, some have diversified into other services such as restaurants or small-scale manufacturing and even export of African crafts (Alden 2007). In contrast to the conviviality experienced by long-established, predominantly Hong Kong migrants, competition, mistrust and division are felt acutely among more recent migrants from mainland China. The Chinese manager of one of his family's electrical fittings shops in Accra highlighted the growing competition brought about by an increase in the number of Chinese traders operating in Ghana in the past few years:

> The competition in China is very, very hard, it is very very big, you know, large and couple of years ago [...] we come out here [...] we can make more money because there is less competition. But this past few years now, there is more Chinese coming out to Ghana and therefore also the competition is getting fiercer as well so your profit is very, very thin now. (Interpreter's translation from Chinese)

Similarly, the Accra-based manager of a Chinese machinery import business mentioned above comments on the intense competition between Chinese traders selling shoes in the city's central market, a sector in which he used to operate: '[I]t's a problem and some they have gone back to China for doing the shoes business. They have more there, I think sixty companies, which is selling shoes in that Makola market. The competition is big.'

Some also fear, or have experience of, being deceived and defrauded by other Chinese migrants. One Chinese shoe wholesaler in Accra said: 'I believe the cheats are many especially Chinese, debtors are a lot; give them money they run away to other countries, they work for about two years then run to another country.' A Hong Kong Chinese entrepreneur who traded in Lagos before establishing a restaurant and distribution business in Kano believes that the increased competition brought about by the growing Chinese presence has also heightened such instances of intra-ethnic deception:

> [N]ow in Lagos the business not easy. No much business can do now. OK not like before, you bring in some goods [...] you go to China market, open a shop you can gain. Now you don't have this kind of chance. So some Chinese will start to cheat Chinese. And the new people come, the Chinese will say we will give you help look for clearing agents or something, will dupe them very

serious. [...] Even before the Chinese also will cheat Chinese.
Cheat the newcomer. Maybe collect your bill loading and go to
clear your goods, your container never come out. They always say
some problem, some problem. Even there is one lady [...] some
people trust her, give her some bill loading to clear the container.
The container clear, she took it. She doesn't give the man and
then give one million to immigration to catch the man and send
him home.

On top of open, price-based competition and deception undermining any sense of a Chinese 'community', there are more subtle
ways in which a lack of trust prevents cooperation. The manager of
a Chinese curtain shop in Accra reported that the competition with
another Chinese curtain shop just down the same street means that
it will not cooperate with him when his supplies run low, explaining:

> If I am going to buy curtain hooks four layer hooks, or single layer
> hook, they won't sell to me [...] we must send some Ghanaians
> to buy. But little by little they will know that these Ghanaians are
> coming from our company [...] But sometimes they also buy
> something from us. Like, er, the rods. We have sold plenty of rods
> to that shop at a cheap price.

Similarly, the Chinese traders in the Lagos China Town show
little cooperation and conviviality. As a Chinese trader based in the
complex said: '[E]verybody here, all Chinese here are taking care of
themselves, protecting their territory but if you have maybe one or
two that will help you but also not too much.'

There are also divides on the bases of cohort, class and region
of origin (Ho 2008; Huynh et al. 2010; Laribee 2008; Park 2010).
Most notable among these is the divide between long-established,
predominantly Hong Kong Chinese industrialists and more recent
arrivals from mainland China, who tend to be associated with the
importation of cheap Chinese products and are seen as a threat
by the long-standing industrialists. For example, the Hong Kong
Chinese manager of her family's struggling textile manufacturing
company in Tema asserted bitterly that the importation of 'cheap'

Chinese-made textiles has been a crippling problem for her company and the wider Ghanaian textile industry over the last ten to fifteen years (Axelsson 2012). A long-established Taiwanese manufacturer in Tema complained that recently arrived Chinese traders not only bring in low-quality goods but also do business without the proper documentation, such as the appropriate visas, meaning that all people of Chinese ethnicity now suffer increased harassment from local officials, especially immigration. She added that recent Chinese migrants are also bringing in young women to work as prostitutes and spend a lot of their money in casinos, her concern seeming to be that they were undermining the respectable reputation of the established ethnic Chinese presence (cf. Park 2009).

This indicates how economic competition can be reflected in cultural labelling with the mainland newcomers sometimes seen as less sophisticated, underhand in their business dealings, and driven by short-term profit seeking. In turn, some of the more recent arrivals from mainland China complained that the established Hong Kong community has done nothing to assist them and has even worked to undermine them. For example, the founder of the Lagos China Town complained that the long-standing Hong Kong Chinese manufacturers do not like to share business ideas with him and his fellow mainland Chinese entrepreneurs, while one of the Chinese traders in his complex explained:

> [B]efore China did her Open Door policy they had Hong Kong people, they had Taiwan people coming to Nigeria to have factories. And along the line those factories became moribund and then when China had their Open Door policy then [mainland Chinese traders] were able to come into Nigeria with goods that are affordable to the Nigerian people and then those Hong Kong factories and those Taiwanese factories complained [...] and what the Nigerian government did was to prohibit lots and lots of goods. (Interpreter's translation from Chinese)

Independent Chinese migrants from mainland China do not form obvious business alliances with the traders in the same line of business. In terms of more formalized modes of cooperation, such as Chambers of Commerce, their connections are even more tenuous. While one of the Chinese Chambers of Commerce in Lagos is headed by a Chinese entrepreneur and seeks to represent main-landers, many migrants of this cohort have little active involvement in such organizations. Some said the Chambers of Commerce tend to be for big businesses and are dominated by the most successful and well-established migrants. Furthermore, they are often seen to be about promoting the particular interests of elite members of the 'community'. When asked if there is any association representing Chinese businesses in Nigeria, the Chinese manager of a Lagos-based firm said:

> Yes we get it but this one not very strong. So if we meet a problem we have to follow the Nigerian custom, follow their way. If the association, that is the first problem, we also we can't trust them very well. At first if we join association we should pay first, we don't know if we meet problem they can protect us or not, we don't know [...] we get an association but not everybody want to join it [...] the bigger company they have good relationship with the Embassy so they will be the member of [the association]. But for the small, small companies, the private company they won't, they can't be joining them, joining that association.

Another reason cited for being reluctant to gather and socialize is that migrants feel they would attract the attention of local officials. For example, the Chinese manager of an electrical equipment outlet in Kano said: '[W]e don't want to, if we gather together and more easy to be found. It's no good because like a police [...] and revenue officer they always trouble us, this is the problem.' The same informant also said that being able to communicate by ICT seems to provide a solution by enabling them to socialize without needing to physically meet.

In summary, our data indicate that networks, cooperation and conviviality tend to feature among the principally Hong Kong Chinese migrants who have been in Africa for more than one generation. Conviviality also features in the social life of the migrants who are employed to work in Africa, perhaps due to the fact that their working environment is not marked by strong competition. In contrast to these two groups of migrants, life in Africa for the independent migrants who operate retail and wholesale businesses tends to be much more competitive and lacking in strong social bonds.

Struggling for success: the mixed fortunes of Chinese migrants in Africa

Transnational Chinese enterprises, both in Africa and beyond, are often associated with business success. Our attitude survey showed that 48 per cent of Ghanaian respondents and 32 per cent of Nigerian respondents felt that Chinese shops were more successful than local ones. The follow-up interviews revealed some of the perceived reasons for relative success and often highlighted a tireless work ethic (see also Park 2010). For example, a Ghanaian male mechanic in Takoradi claimed: 'The Chinese work like machine that I must be frank. I know I work very hard but they can work even harder than I do.' Technological superiority was also seen to be a factor, as a Ghanaian male working as a local government officer in Takoradi argued: 'The Chinese are [more] technologically advanced than Ghanaians and hence they want to use that to their advantage. This they do in a way by bringing in their improvised technology.' However, while 27 per cent of Nigerian and 18 per cent of Ghanaian respondents put the success of Chinese shops down to the fact that the Chinese 'work harder', more saw access to cheap goods as their real competitive advantage (around 40 per cent of respondents in both countries).

The issue of the work ethic is revisited later, but there is a strong tendency for both Chinese and African respondents to see the Chinese approach as superior, though not all agree. The issue of superior technology was also played out many times and was linked to relative stages of development, with China seen as 'more advanced' than Africa.

Certainly the misconception of China as the 'new imperialist' in Africa is premised on an assumed vigour in Chinese commercial activity, frequently linked to a more disciplined work ethic. We found cases of business expansion and success, and some Hong Kong manufacturers in Nigeria are well known for this. The most successful of these have also been able to educate their children in the West and retire in comfort. The lifestyle of the Kano-based Hong Kong Chinese couple mentioned above is typical of the successful second-generation Chinese migrants. They have a couple of properties in central London and they and their children have Canadian citizenship. Both of their children have studied in the UK. The son is a medical doctor and the daughter is a lawyer but neither choses to live in Nigeria. The couple spend their time travelling between London, Hong Kong, Canada and Kano.

However, there are also many who are struggling to succeed. Indeed, what might at first appear as the rapid and unproblematic expansion of the Chinese entrepreneurial presence masks many failures and a high turnover of migrants. There is a sense that the moment at which Africa represents a clear economic opportunity for some lines of business, particularly trading, can soon pass as competition from other Chinese entrepreneurs increases (Haugen and Carling 2005). Speaking about the lack of continuity and longevity of the businesses in the Lagos China Town, a Chinese entrepreneur based in the complex said:

> Most Chinese big traders have left. What remain now [...] are small trade [...] most people [...] the one came before me, or before 2004 [...] most people has left. [...] Even last year, the people came last year, they left. I am sure after this December, after Christmas I am sure many Chinese here, they are losing money. I am sure losing so 50 per cent will go [...] so that is what is happening.

When asked about the reason for such a high turnover, the same informant said: '[T]hat time [in the past] not many Nigerians, but now trading is done by Nigerians [...] Chinese don't have advantage to this trading. Because for Chinese to do trading the cost is more, much more than Nigerians.' Some informants talked about corruption as a contributing factor to the difficulties they face. As we saw above, it is claimed that goods containers arriving at the Lagos port sometimes disappear, regardless of whether or not the owner has the correct paperwork.

Some of our informants said that the profit margin of their businesses is minimal or they just about break even. However, they cannot pull out quickly because the majority of their capital is tied up in goods in transit or goods in warehouses. Rents for business premises are often paid in advance. While they felt the business environment is challenging, they did not have a better option. When asked whether he operates at a loss sometimes, a trader in the Lagos China Town said:

> [W]e cannot just leave when we want to. It takes time to wrap business up. Sometimes I really want to leave, but my money is tied up in the next shipment. So you just have to wait until your container arrives then you have to try to sell the contents of the container. Once you have money, you have to pay your debt, your employees, then your money runs out, so you have to continue to source goods and send containers.

These informants are often in an unhappy limbo.

On the social side, younger informants looking after family businesses in Lagos China Town talked of boredom. Of those who came to Africa on their own, some experience social isolation. We came across a number of Chinese migrants working for Chinese restaurants. Some of the employers (both Chinese and Africans) pay for fares and visa applications and become the employees' sponsors. When the employees arrive they are bound to work for the sponsors for a contractual period; some respondents suggested that sponsors hold the passports of their employees to ensure that they do not work for anyone else or change their minds and abscond to return to China.

As discussed, many migrants working in Africa are separated from their families. A Lagos-based Hong Kong Chinese restaurant manager who eventually followed his father to Nigeria told us his early life was marked by separation from his father: '[My] father [...] came to Nigeria in 1959 [...] I was only three years old. After I was three I did not see my father [...] because of work.' This informant's experience of separation is by no means an isolated case. Those who have children often cited a lack of good healthcare and good schools as reasons for not having their families with them. Those informants whose spouses have jobs in China said it was important to keep two jobs because jobs are difficult to come by due to competition in China. Therefore, separation from their families is seen a sacrifice that is necessary in order to maintain income streams and raise a family.

Fortunately, for some of the families, separation is only temporary. We found a small number of examples of women and their children moving to Africa to be reunited with their husbands and fathers. In Angola, we found wives of middle-level management personnel moving to join them after a couple of months. They subsequently found work within the same company. In Ghana, there were cases of family members, such as sisters and children, who have moved to Accra to reunite with their brothers and fathers after two years of separation.

Conclusion

In this chapter, we have outlined the extent to which the economic organization of Chinese migrants matches the key features as outlined in the literature on Chinese capitalism and ethnic economy. Although networks of family and personal relationships are important in some instances, other factors are equally, if not more, pertinent in particular contexts. Certainly, some firms were family-based and used various family members, but recruitment was also done through agencies on the basis of competitive interviews. Moreover, most labour in these firms is African. Additionally, while Chinese family firms are assumed to operate with strict gender hierarchies, we found cases where spouses had relatively equal roles and where it was women who had driven the migration; this may be linked to the legacy of Maoism in instigating a culture of separation, enduring hardship and women's autonomy. We also showed that while broad-based Chinese organizations existed to foment trade and cultural integration, the level of community cohesion among Chinese migrants was quite low and supports the work of Ho (2008) in this regard.

While formal community organization was patchy, we did find virtual communities of Chinese based in a particular African country as well as websites dedicated to would-be migrants to Africa. These not only function as mechanisms to exchange information but serve, in some cases, as a means to escape the apparent boredom of residing in Africa and to enable socializing. Finally, while most of the literature on Chinese migrants as transnational capitalists assumes that these businesses are only ever successful, we argued that the risks involved in coming to Africa are high, the realities of an expatriate life can be hard and a number of ventures fail. Part of the difficulty of living and working in Africa is expressed as tensions and conflicts and it is to these that we now turn.

5 | CONSTRUCTING THE OTHER: NARRATIVES OF TENSION AND CONFLICT IN SINO-AFRICAN ENCOUNTERS

Introduction

In accounts of the growing Chinese presence in Africa, a particular concern has been how and with what effects Chinese migrants interact with their 'host' societies. Most attention on this topic has been devoted to the apparent conflicts that have developed (Trofimov 2007). The most notable case has been that of Zambia, where the issue of Chinese traders taking over key sections of the economy became a central part of Michael Sata's presidential campaign in 2006. Tensions have been reported in various African localities, usually in connection with trading, health and safety issues, or illegal mining and there have been a range of protests by groups such as market traders and mine workers. The response by more organized civil society has been mixed, though some trade unions have undertaken research into labour practices and wage levels in Chinese firms. In all these cases the western media and international non-governmental organizations (NGOs) have helped to elevate these issues beyond the immediate locality where the grievance occurred and fed the wider perception of 'Chinese capitalism' as particularly venal and brutal. In arguing that this international involvement has escalated the issue, we are not defending the actions of Chinese firms, but the point is that selective media reporting tends to portray the tensions as evidence of Chinese exploitation. In this chapter we want to delve deeper into the tensions by looking at their source, how they are being expressed and with what political consequences.

This chapter, and the theory that underpins much of it, is linked to the next chapter, which examines the more convivial relations between Chinese migrants and their hosts. So, these are effectively a pair – this chapter exploring tensions and Chapter 6 nuancing these accounts of apparent conflict. One of the key issues in these two chapters is the interplay of multiple social differences using the ideas of intersectionality. The complexity of the factors shaping these tensions, their subtlety and, at times, contradictions mean that we cannot use the lens of race or nationality to explain what we found. Rather, we have combined axes of social difference in context-specific cases to tease out the interplay of forces. The other important upshot of this is that we move away from seeing what Chinese migrants do in Africa as exceptional and different from what other people vying for Africa's resources, now or in the past, have done. That is, we need to be specific about what is unique to the China–Africa relationship and differentiate this from what is part of a broader pattern of external engagements with the continent. And ultimately we want to say what this means for African development, since simply pointing out that the Chinese are 'no worse' or 'just the same' as western actors does not really bode well for Africa's future.

The structure of this chapter is mirrored in the next. We begin by reviewing the underpinning theory before examining three sites of tension in this chapter and three sites of conviviality in the next. In this chapter the next section develops ideas about migrant integration and intersectionality. Then there is a section on how Chinese migrants perceive their personal safety in Africa as a powerful reason for their feelings of anxiety towards their hosts. After that we examine economic sectors where competition between Chinese and African businesses largely explains the source of tensions. The penultimate section moves from the sectoral to the intra-firm level where we look at the relationships between employers and employees. As noted, most attention has focused on the poor pay and conditions offered by Chinese employers but we also show that some Africans are employing Chinese workers, which has released a backlash by organized labour. We conclude with a thematic summary.

Migration, integration and marginalization

In seeking to understand the root causes and effects of these tensions, we need to situate these sentiments in longer histories of identity and senses of nationhood in both China and those African countries we are dealing with here. For example, Dikkoter (1992) has talked about how a particular sense of racial superiority can be found in China, but that this is also a dynamic and relational sense (see also Nyíri 2006). In African polities we also have ethnicized groups and debates about autochthony (Geschiere and Nyamnjoh 2000) as well as long-standing processes of global engagement, forced or otherwise (Bayart 2000). Expressions of racial difference or outright xenophobia are clearly not unique to the presence of Chinese migrants in Africa, nor are they confined to obvious racial difference since prejudice can be against 'foreigners' who are of the same racial background (Kirshner 2012). While the phenomenon of racial prejudice around the world is rightfully linked to economic marginalization (Gilroy 1987), it is not enough to argue that poverty alone explains antagonism to 'outsiders'. As Kirshner (2012) argues in the context of xenophobia in South Africa, whether in-migration to relatively poor areas incites racial tensions is also shaped by state discourses and practices, as well as the nature of local informal politics where, in some parts of South Africa, parallel leadership structures have a determining role in the reception of immigrants. Hence, in both the Chinese and African cases, in addition to economic factors we also need to consider how formal and informal politics of different sorts play into the reception of migrants, and how these are shaped by other axes of social difference.

In thinking through this interplay of 'class' and 'culture', we have to examine the complex 'coupling' of different facets of identity and social positioning. By doing this we do not take at face value the stereotypical pronouncements of our respondents. We do need to take these expressed sentiments seriously but we also have to go deeper to ascertain how far they mask other axes of socio-economic difference and what these other axes might mean.

One aspect of the debate surrounding intersectionality, which we outlined in the opening chapter, is the additive problem; namely, that there are multiple axes of difference so that it is somewhat arbitrary to stop 'adding' ever more complex mixtures of social categories. In trying to analyse these complex intersections of social difference we are guided by the idea that the processes that create difference are both '*co-constitutive* [...] and as *distinctive* and historically specific technologies of categorization' (Nash 2008: 13, emphasis in original). Hence, we cannot essentialize social categories and simply add them up to determine the degree of oppression, but rather examine 'how specific social positionings and (not necessarily corresponding) identities and political values are constructed and interrelate and affect each other in particular locations and contexts' (Yuval-Davis 2006: 200). While most theorists of intersectionality avoid prescribing which social differences are necessarily important and rightly follow Yuval-Davis's empirical call for 'particular locations and contexts', some social divisions tend to be found across cases, namely age, gender, ethnicity, class and life cycle stage. So, in any given spatial and temporal context, some differences are more important than others (Phoenix and Pattynama 2006).

An important issue for this book is whether intersectionality applies only to the oppressed or is a more general framework for analysing social complexity. Given its roots in critical race and gender studies, most uses of intersectionality have examined processes of deprivation and marginality but arguably it could be used to look at relative privilege (Nash 2008) or empowerment (Davis 2008; Bürkner 2012). Given that social dimensions are relational, then, while we need to avoid simplistic zero-sum analysis, any act of oppression will produce privilege such that understanding privilege is part and parcel of the seemingly more progressive act of identifying oppression. In a given case, as Nash (2008: 12) postulates, a person 'might be both victimized by patriarchy and privileged by race', though the logic could apply to other combinations of social difference. Hence in this and the next chapter we examine complex positionings of 'the Chinese' as sometimes privileged by their class position vis-à-vis their African employees but also as subject to racial stereotyping and discrimination.

In the context of this study we focus on a broadly middle-class group of Chinese migrants. This had not been an explicit aim of the research project; rather, those Chinese migrants we encountered tended to be from this class background. Interest in the middle classes has seen something of a revival in development studies in the last few years (Lawson 2012: Ballard 2012), though much of this focuses on their aspirational culture and consumption as a driver of imports and production. As Lawson (2012: 4) notes, regarding much of the work in development studies on poverty, it 'depoliticizes poverty by obscuring the ways in which more powerful people benefit from the workings of capitalist markets and neoliberal governance'. Her team's approach is to look both intersectionally and relationally at classes and to see the middle classes as having class agency in their own right as opposed to simply being a buffer or residual category between elites and subaltern classes. But as Das (2012) notes in his re-emphasis of Marxist class analysis, we need to avoid a focus on single classes as acting independently of the wider system of exploitation and accumulation of which they are a part. In this sense, agency is not boundless.

In terms of specific contexts we certainly found that some notable areas of tension and conflict have developed in both Ghana and Nigeria (and Angola). Three of the most prominent areas concern the corruption and crime experienced by Chinese migrants; the activities of Chinese traders in the informal retail sector; and the treatment of local workers in Chinese enterprises as well as the place of Chinese workers in 'African' businesses. In each case and on both sides, there is some evidence of negative, racialized stereotypes emerging, potentially creating a distinct and dangerous divide that could be exploited by politicians, as has been seen in Zambia. Here we explore how and to what extent such a divide has developed.

Tension and conflict I: Chinese migrants versus crime and corruption

From the perspective of Chinese respondents, African 'host' societies can often appear hostile and even dangerous, with a number of challenges making settlement and everyday life difficult. Principal among these are crime and corruption, and there is some sense that Chinese people are specifically targeted as a visible 'foreign' community that is often seen to have money (Carling and Haugen 2008; Park 2010). There is particular concern about 'armed robbery', especially in Nigeria, with several respondents giving alarming first- and second-hand accounts. For example, the Hong Kong Chinese manager of an up-market Chinese restaurant in Lagos recalled: 'Seventeen armed robber came to my restaurant [...] and put their AK-47 on my head. In Nigeria this is the third time, the third time AK-47 on my head!' While Ghana is generally seen to be considerably safer than Nigeria, armed robbery still tends to be regarded as a prominent threat, with anxieties raised at the time of our fieldwork by a spate of attacks that occurred in Tema during 2010, in which several Chinese businesses were targeted. A Chinese restaurateur based in the city told us that it was 'not safe' and reported that most of the Chinese restaurants there had been robbed, including hers – a Chinese customer had US$20,000 stolen which he had been carrying to buy equipment for his new gold-mining venture.

Such instances of armed robbery appear to have a wider effect on the social and economic activities of Chinese migrants. Some Chinese respondents highlighted the fear of serious crime as a key factor discouraging social interaction with their co-nationals. For example, a Tema-based Hong Kong Chinese manufacturer who arrived in Ghana in the late 1980s bemoaned the fact that it was no longer safe enough for him and his wife to go out in the evenings to meet their Hong Kong Chinese friends, reducing their socializing to daytime meetings on Sundays. Expressing his frustration at the Ghanaian government for failing to ensure basic security, he argued that this was not only a problem for him and his co-nationals but also for the Ghanaian economy. He reasoned that curtailing their social lives reduced the amount of money they spend in the country. Indeed, the economic implications could be much greater than this; it was suggested that concerns about armed robbery could deter long-term Chinese settlement and investment. The Chinese manager of a Lagos-based Chinese manufacturing company, who has himself been a victim of armed robbery on five occasions since arriving in Nigeria in 2003, contended that armed criminals are 'terrorizing' the country, causing some Chinese people to leave. Highlighting a recent attack on a Chinese trading company, in which over US$5,000 was stolen and a Chinese person was wounded with a machete, an executive of one of the two main Chinese associations in Lagos argued that 'lack of security' and 'fear' are the primary reasons why many recent Chinese entrepreneurial migrants to Nigeria have established trading enterprises rather than making longer-term investments in manufacturing. '[E]very time you have armed robbers coming to attack the Chinese traders,' he contended, '[there will be] no spirit of continuity or long time stay in them' (interpreter's translation from Chinese). For Chinese entrepreneurs based in Ghana who are tempted by the larger market in Nigeria, this perceived lack of security in the larger neighbour is often cited as a key reason why they have been deterred from even attempting to invest there.

While there is particular concern about armed robbery, it is only one of a number of criminal threats that are posed by the 'host' society. As has been suggested elsewhere in Africa (McNamee et al. 2012), there are some complaints from Chinese migrants about stealing by local staff, though such practices are not confined to Chinese firms. For the Chinese manager of an import outlet in Accra, this is a source of notable irritation, particularly from his domestic staff.

> [T]hey will steal your things. This one every time I have to put an eye, keep my eye on them. I have to tell them don't do this again, because I'm afraid if I bring another house girl [...] the same thing will happen. So always I have to tell him and persuade him what he should do, what he shouldn't do.

For a Hong Kong Chinese entrepreneur in Kano, stealing by local staff has been a more serious problem. She lamented that local staff stealing money and supplies from her restaurant makes running the business 'very, very difficult' and recalled bitterly that in her original trading business, her local employees stole almost all the profit, partly by not handing over the cash they received from sales.

What comes across as a wider threat in terms of Africans dishonestly extracting wealth from Chinese enterprises is local duplicity in business transactions. Prominent here are complaints about local customers not paying for goods, especially when sold on credit. For example, a Chinese textile trader in Kano admitted 'day by day there are many bad debts you cannot collect back', while a Chinese entrepreneur based in the Lagos China Town reported that there were local customers who have 'refused to pay the Chinese', adding:

[E]ven my customer [...] I have this kind of problem, that's why for now, [business is] not moving. What we are doing is cash directly, [if customers have] no cash, we cannot sell. If we sell with credit that means probably the money will go, you will not get it back, that's the risk in this place.

A well-established Chinese entrepreneur who is heavily involved in Chinese community organizing in Lagos even argues that it is Nigerian importers and traders not paying for goods ordered from China that has compelled many Chinese suppliers to come and trade directly in Nigeria. Indeed, asserting that 'you can't trust' some local entrepreneurs because they are 'phoney', a Lagos-based Chinese factory manager suggested that the 'danger' of Nigerian importers not paying for their shipments was a factor in his company's decision to open an assembly and sales operation in Nigeria itself, while the Kano-based Hong Kong Chinese trader noted above reported:

I opened a trading [company] in China but lose money. Sometimes the Nigeria[ns] purchase and then the container put in the warehouse and they don't pay it. [...S]o lose money and then that's why I say I come here, I bring container, come here and then I want get back my money.

Some Chinese respondents also highlighted similar problems with local suppliers. There is some annoyance at the tendency of locals to try and charge foreigners considerably higher prices for goods and services. However, the main frustration is that contracts are not always fulfilled. For example, a Chinese entrepreneur who left a state-owned enterprise to establish a travel agency in Lagos claimed that his mostly Chinese clientele often came to him because they had had enough of being 'duped' by Nigerian travel agents. Similarly, a well-established Kano-based Chinese restaurateur asserted that recent arrivals regularly turn to him for immigration and business registration advice as local lawyers just 'chop' their money. ('Chop' is Nigerian Pidgin for 'eat' and is often used to refer to embezzlement.)

This restaurateur complained that he had his own problems with local suppliers, having had to abandon a cocoa and cashew nut export business when his local supplier started 'cheating' him by using stones to bulk up the bags of produce he was selling. And in the Lagos China Town, a Chinese trader reported that she and her fellow Chinese traders in the complex had had some especially challenging experiences with local clearing agents upon whom they depend to navigate their shipments of goods through local ports, though again this is not unique to Chinese traders (Chalfin 2008): '[S]ome agent carry your container out, but they run away sell for somebody, sell big money and run away.' While she has since found a reliable local clearing agent, she readily recalled how the resulting loss of money pushed her trading business to the edge of survival, leaving her unable to sleep and losing her hair because of the worry.

Some particularly stressful and damaging experiences of under-hand business practices are also reported in relation to working with local partners. A Chinese entrepreneur based in Lagos lamented that he had twice attempted to go into manufacturing but failed each time, blaming one of these failures on a Nigerian partner who apparently 'drained' all the capital and charged three times the actual cost for building the joint-venture's factory. Similarly, a long-established Hong Kong Chinese businesswoman based in Ghana recounted with huge regret that her and her husband's first main business, a manu-facturing company, ran into difficulties several years ago and was subsequently sold off by their Ghanaian partner who, she said, gave them only a relatively small payment from the sale. This precipitated something of a tirade about local duplicity, including an account of how their attempt to start a food-processing company was under-mined by a local partner stealing the business. Clearly deeply upset by these experiences, she complained that they had lost all their money in Ghana.

However, for most Chinese respondents, a more common and frustrating problem is what they see as harassment and extortion by corrupt local officials. While there is some acknowledgement that a good number of their co-nationals may not be in full compli-ance with local regulations, there is a strong and widespread sense among them that the frequent attention of local officials tends to be motivated primarily by a desire to extract unofficial and often unjustified payments rather than enforce the law. For example, a Chinese restaurateur in Tema complained that, despite having all her documentation in order when she opened her business, she was met with a series of visits by officials from the immigration, revenue and municipal authorities who showed little interest in any kind of inspection and just wanted money. Similarly, a Chinese entrepreneur based in the Lagos China Town remarked:

> I used to go outside with car. When police catch me they will hold my driving licence, he will now ask for, even I don't have any problems, he will ask for money [...] That's why I will always be afraid if I see police or LASTMA [Lagos State Traffic Management Authority], [...] what they want is money, big money.

Like the fear of armed robbery, concerns about harassment and corruption from local officials are seen by some Chinese respondents to constrain social life and deter economic investment. Reflecting this, the Kano-based Hong Kong Chinese entrepreneur mentioned above contended:

> [T]he immigration, they always come out to catch people. Even go to restaurant, so the Chinese scare to come out. Sometimes they catch them, ask 500, 5,000 US dollar. [...] So people scared to come out so their lifestyle change. They go to this family's house, gather together and limit the times come out.

The Chinese manager of an electrical equipment outlet in Kano concurred, and added that such actions on the part of officials 'block social development' by discouraging foreign investors. Furthermore, it would seem that they also contribute to a general sense among many Chinese migrants that their Africa 'host' societies can represent threatening, sometimes dangerous environments in which to live and work.

Such sentiments are set against quite contrasting views from Africans. Around 30 per cent of Nigerians felt that the Chinese succeeded because the Chinese government helped them, which comes from the belief – not confined to Nigerians – that the Chinese state orchestrates all of the activities of Chinese businesses. And while some Chinese business people cited petty corruption as a source of threat or insecurity, equally some African respondents saw Chinese traders as flouting local laws. For example, a Ghanaian male working as a spare parts dealer in Accra contended:

> Maybe there are loopholes in the investment code that they have taken advantage of and that is why they are trooping into the country day in day out. Because they may come in as visitors or tourists but as soon as they gain entry permit, tomorrow you find them engaging in some activities.

As Lee (2007) notes, such perceptions of bypassing local laws are often cited as a reason why some Africans feel the Chinese are more successful and feed into a desire for tighter enforcement of existing regulations.

Tension and conflict II: Chinese traders versus African traders and manufacturers

It has been well documented that the growing Chinese presence in Africa has generated considerable public debate and even protest. As in a number of other African countries (see, e.g., Dittgen 2010; Dobler 2008; McNamee et al. 2012; Scheld 2011), one of the most contentious issues related to the Chinese presence in Ghana and Nigeria is the arrival since the early 2000s of significant numbers of Chinese traders and their importation of large quantities of 'cheap' Chinese consumer goods. This is often seen to present a direct challenge to locals operating in the informal retail sector and to undermine local manufacturing.

While African survey respondents speaking as consumers generally bought Chinese goods on price, they also cited quality as a factor. But in the follow-up interviews there was a greater awareness shown of substandard products, or at least items aimed at poorer consumers. As a Nigerian student in Lagos claimed: 'I have bought a China phone before that didn't last up to a month.' There is a realization that not only do these goods break easily, but that this negatively impacts on 'our' goods and can put African firms out of business. For example, a Lagos-based Nigerian teacher contended: '[N]obody is patronizing our local goods because of the China product so because of that now you have to go for what you feel is cheap and you feel they are importing it from abroad then you forget or relegate our goods to the background.' Similarly, a Ghanaian businessman in Accra complained:

> [T]hey come and take over our product and trade as we are doing. A time may come that we cannot get anything doing and they will repatriate their profit back to their country. With my sector it has taken many people out of business except we who go and come and get new products all the time.

In Ghana, some of the most prominent agitation against the Chinese trading presence has been led by the Ghana Union of Traders' Associations (GUTA) and has centred on the main markets of central Accra. Shops run by Chinese traders started to become a notable feature of central Accra in the early 2000s, especially in the vicinity of a large retail complex in Rawlings Park which was emblazoned as the 'Ghana Chinese Commodities Wholesale Town' around 2004 and is popularly known as 'China Town', even though only a few Chinese shops remain in the complex. By late 2005, GUTA began expressing its dissatisfaction with the 'unrestrained invasion' of 'foreigners' into the retail sector and suggested that a 'massive demonstration' would be held in Accra if the government failed to enforce the 1994 Ghana Investment Promotion Centre (GIPC) Act (Takyi-Boadu 2005). This legislation explicitly reserves for Ghanaians the business of retailing in public markets and stipulates that any form of foreign-owned trading enterprise must make a minimum investment of US$300,000 and employ at least ten local staff. Although the government was aware of the growing disquiet and had already undertaken to review the legislation (GNA 2005), its response failed to satisfy GUTA. In late 2007, the association organized a day of action involving the closure of shops and a march which converged for a mass rally in Opera Square, bringing the capital's commercial heart to a standstill (GNA 2007a; 2007b; Klutse and Ennin 2007). The government entered into discussions with GUTA and in mid-2009 agreed to revise the GIPC Act and form a multi-agency task force to more effectively enforce the legislation (Nonor 2009).

However, the task force had a limited impact. While the Ghanaian manager of the China Town complex reported that increasing attention from immigration and revenue officials played a role in encouraging most of the Chinese shops to leave the complex, many simply relocated to nearby streets where, dispersed among African businesses, they apparently felt less vulnerable to targeting by the authorities. Indeed, by 2011, some of the side roads and smaller complexes near China Town were almost completely dominated by Chinese shops, many selling shoes with others specializing in luggage, household furnishings, electrical fittings, plumbing equipment and fishing nets.

The GUTA officials we interviewed remained highly agitated, complaining that while the Chinese shops claim to engage only in wholesale, they continue to retail despite being unlikely to have met the legal requirements to make an initial investment of US$300,000 and employ a minimum of ten local workers. Compounding this, GUTA argued, Chinese traders gain unfair advantages through a range of underhand practices such as selling cheaper 'imitation' goods, under-reporting imports and sales to reduce tariffs and taxes, avoiding social security payments for the local staff they employ, and using their greater access to credit to inflate shop rents and force locals out of business (see Lee 2007). The GIPC task force has failed to rectify the situation, GUTA complained, because there is a 'tendency' for officials to take payments from the Chinese shops in return for not enforcing the regulations. While the current Minister for Trade and Industry has publicly sympathized with GUTA's concerns (GNA 2010), officials of the association warn that if decisive action is not taken soon, they may no longer be able to contain the frustration of their members. '[I]f nothing is done about it,' the GUTA General Secretary contended, '[...] every human endurance has its limit, so when it reaches the peak, definitely there will be eruption.' Indeed, he went on to report that a branch of GUTA recently put forward a resolution threatening direct action against Chinese traders: 'If nothing is done about it, perhaps we will come and flush them out ourselves.'

In Nigeria, strong resistance to the activities of Chinese traders has also been excited by the emergence of a prominent China Town shopping complex. Nigeria's first China Town had originally been established in 1999 in the up-market Lagos district of Ikoyi but in 2002 it began to relocate to a larger site in Ojota. By this time, China Town had become a target for prominent Nigerian manufacturers, and the Manufacturers Association of Nigeria (MAN) argued that the complex was a channel for the influx of cheap and often sub-standard Chinese consumer goods which were undermining local producers, particularly in the textile industry (see also Akinrinade and Ogen 2008; Ogidan 2004). Responding to these calls from the manufacturing lobby, the Federal Government added a new raft of goods, including textiles, to its import prohibition list and in late 2005, just nine months after the new China Town was officially commissioned, officers of the Nigeria Customs Service raided the complex, seized contraband goods and sealed the premises (Obasola 2006). 'The activities of foreigners should not be allowed to destroy the industrial base of this country,' declared the head of the Customs Service (quoted in Mbachu 2006: 81). MAN promptly commended the government for taking action and called for those involved in selling prohibited goods to be prosecuted and the China Town to be closed permanently (*Daily Independent* 2006; Okere 2006).

While no prosecutions appear to have been made and the complex was allowed to reopen three months later (Obasola 2006), interviews with China Town management and traders indicate that the raid and temporary closure severely disrupted its activities, with most of the Chinese traders losing large amounts of stock and many seeking alternative opportunities elsewhere in Nigeria and beyond. Those who remained in the Lagos China Town and continued to import contraband goods, particularly textiles, found it increasingly expensive to 'settle' officials and even then often had their shipments confiscated. Business never recovered to the previous levels, and at the time of research almost half the complex's shops were un-occupied. For their part, the MAN officials we interviewed certainly appeared to be less concerned about the specific case of China Town and more inclined to focus their efforts on the wider problem of regulating the importation of counterfeit and substandard Chinese goods. The activities of Chinese traders have nevertheless continued to be a cause of local agitation, particularly in Kano's textile market where complaints about a growing Chinese presence in direct retailing recently prompted the arrest of forty-five Chinese traders by the Nigeria Immigration Service, the local Immigration Service chief promising that they would be deported and declaring that 'economic scavengers' would not be allowed in Nigeria (BBC 2012).

Tension and conflict III: Chinese and African bosses versus African and Chinese workers

Alongside the activities of Chinese migrant traders, a third issue in debates about the growing Chinese presence in Africa has been the employment of locals in Chinese enterprises. Much has been made of the apparent tendency of Chinese companies in Africa to import most of their labour from China and thereby create relatively few opportunities for local employment (see, e.g., Bergesen 2008). However, while there have been some Chinese state-backed projects in Ghana and Nigeria where a large proportion of the labour has been Chinese, this has not emerged as the major area of concern for employment. Indeed, with Chinese enterprises in the two countries often employing largely African workforces, it is relations between Chinese bosses and their local workers that have become the over-riding issue.

From the perspective of Chinese employers, working with local labour is often represented as a difficult and frustrating experience. Underpinning these narratives is a widespread sense that local labour has a number of limitations, especially when compared with Chinese labour. These differences are often seen to be culturally embedded (see also Carling and Haugen 2008), resulting in some negative, racialized stereotyping of local workers by Chinese bosses. A prominent complaint is that local employees are generally not hard-working, dedicated or productive, with some Chinese employers claiming that local workers tend to be 'slow' or 'lazy'. For example, a long-established Chinese manufacturer based in Tema contended that finding good local workers was 'a lot of problem', adding: 'Ghanaians [...] excuse me to saying that a lot of them they are very lazy. [...] The way how they work [...] so slow. They can take from here, take a walk to the production floor, just about a few seconds, they can take for two or three minutes.'

Such claims are linked to assertions that local workers frequently fail to complete tasks when asked and have a tendency to defer work. As a Lagos-based Chinese entrepreneur complained: '[T]he Chinese have a custom which is what can be done today should be done today [...] But unfortunately [...] the Nigerian mentality is that everything is always pushed until tomorrow [...] nothing ever gets done today' (Interpreter's translation from Chinese). A lack of commitment was also felt to be evident in the lateness and absenteeism sometimes associated with local workers. For example, a Chinese restaurant manager in Kano contended: 'Sometimes your staff, if he wants to work today he will come, tomorrow if he doesn't feel like working, he will not come.' Similarly, a Chinese shop manager in Accra reported: '[T]he locals' working habit is unpredictable [...] today maybe ten workers will come [...] tomorrow maybe five will come' (Interpreter's translation from Chinese). Furthermore, the Tema-based Chinese manufacturer quoted above argued that there was a particular and widespread problem of local employees not turning up for work the day after they receive their monthly salary.

Local workers are also criticized for lacking initiative and needing constant supervision. For instance, the Chinese manager of a retail outlet in Accra remarked:

Sometimes they cannot do what you are seeking. Like, for example, I want them to do that but I didn't tell them, this they should realize by themselves. [...] But they have to let me to tell, to push. Some things I think, OK, that thing they have seen so they will do [it], I don't need to talk to them, that they will do by themselves. But no, I have to talk, I have to tell them you should do that, you should do this.

However, what is often considered especially frustrating, and strikingly different from what is seen as the cultural norm in China, is local workers' unwillingness to work beyond normal hours, even when financial incentives are offered. As an Accra-based Chinese shop manager contended:

> The working experience between China and Ghana is completely different. In China we like to work [...] And we don't mind working overtime, we don't mind working at weekends. We can work from morning till 10pm without any break [...] But in Ghana it's different. [...] they don't want to work overtime, they don't want to work on weekends. (Interpreter's translation from Chinese)

As has been highlighted elsewhere in Africa (see, e.g., Brooks 2010; Baah and Jauch 2009; Lee 2009), there are widespread complaints about low pay and poor conditions in Chinese companies and a growing sense in some quarters that the Chinese are particularly bad employers (Human Rights Watch 2011). Our attitude survey showed that 44 per cent of Ghanaian respondents and 50 per cent of Nigerian respondents felt that Chinese employers were worse than local employers, but this was based on a small sub-sample of those who had worked for a Chinese company and so cannot be seen as statistically robust. In the follow-up interviews of those with more direct knowledge of the Chinese we found mixed opinions. One recurring trope was that the Chinese were hard-working, but that they also expected a lot from their employees and were poor payers. Typical is a Ghanaian male respondent in Takoradi who said the average Chinese boss 'sees you as not in to help the business but relates to him as a slave and he the master' and a Nigerian male respondent in Lagos echoed this: 'Chinese people are the type that still view the blacks as slaves.' However, a 24-year-old Ghanaian woman who works as an administrator in Accra and had worked with a Chinese company observed: 'The Chinese tend to be hard, strict compared to the typical Ghanaian employer. The Chinese are hard-working, punctual and they don't joke with their work compared to a typical Ghanaian employer.' These quotes capture the two shades of opinion – that the Chinese are hierarchical and abusive or that they are strict but that this reflects their own approach to work.

GUTA certainly echoes the more negative accusations in its case against Chinese traders operating in Accra's markets. An official of the association argued: '[T]hey go in for cheap labour, people who do not even know let alone understand their rights, then they will take them as temporary [workers], under-pay them, then they discard them after some time and then recruit another.' A Ghanaian who has for several years helped some of these Chinese traders with their accounts and tax returns, and who appears to have no particular grudge against them, concurs, describing the wages they pay their local shop staff as 'very woeful'. 'They don't pay much at all,' he contended, 'aside that he will not pay any social security, he will just not pay anything for you. They can also just decide to just let you go anytime he feels he doesn't want your services.'

Having experienced such conditions, a Ghanaian worker in a Chinese shop in Accra complained that his salary of around 80 cedis a month barely covered his basic living expenses. He contended that his employers only meet their legal obligation to pay his social security contributions because he asked them to do so and he was particularly angry that they deduct his pay when he is unable to attend work due to illness. For him, such treatment is symptomatic of a general lack of basic respect and compassion on the part of Chinese bosses. 'They don't care about black [people],' he lamented bitterly. 'They don't care about you the worker, he doesn't even respect you.' This illustrates not only how the treatment of local workers in Chinese enterprises can generate anger and resentment but also how this can be expressed in racialized ways, instigating a process of othering through which distinct and potentially divisive identity boundaries are constructed (cf. Giese and Thiel 2012). The Ghanaian worker continued: 'I have worked with these people, I know how they are [...] So as for me I look at them and laugh. I say, "You people, you are very bad people" [...] These Chinese people [...] I don't like them.' And as in the case of GUTA's agitation against Chinese traders, there is an implicit threat of violence contained only by the self-ascribed restraint of Ghanaians: '[Y]ou can see a Chinese man with the money, you can easily beat him and take the money, but we don't do that.'

In Nigeria, controversy about labour conditions in Chinese enterprises has been generated in the manufacturing sector, where a number of long-established Hong Kong Chinese companies have not only become key players but also developed a reputation for poor industrial relations (Mthembu-Salter 2009; Obiorah 2007; Oyeranti et al. 2011; Taylor 2007b; Utomi 2008). The issue of low pay is again to the fore; an official of MAN claimed: 'In fact, they enslave workers, their pay is very, very poor.' This has led to incidents of industrial unrest and this respondent recalled that workers at a well-known Hong Kong Chinese factory in Lagos once became so aggrieved at their low pay that they demonstrated and 'wanted to burn the whole place'. It was also reported that this company upset its workers and the Nigeria Labour Congress by apparently employing people on a casual basis, even after years of service in some cases (Babalola and Lawal 2002; Ibharuneafe 2002a; Oyeranti et al. 2011).

Such tensions arising from pay and casualization have been compounded by the reported anti-union practices of some Chinese manufacturing companies in Nigeria. For example, when the National Union of Chemical, Footwear, Rubber, Leather and Non-Metallic Products Employees (NUCFRLNMPE) called for improvements in workers' conditions at a factory in Kano belonging to one of the two largest Hong Kong Chinese industrial conglomerates based in Nigeria, the company reportedly responded by intimidating union members and temporarily shutting down the factory (Ahiuma-Young 2009; Atomre et al. 2009; *Nation* 2008). A senior NUCFRLNMPE official in Kano lamented that none of the company's factories in the city currently has a branch of the union and that any worker who attempts to form one is promptly sacked. Consequently, he claimed, the company continues to coerce its workers into working excessive hours while paying salaries that can be less than half the negotiated industry-wide minimum monthly wage of NGN13,400.

> This is a document, it's a law [...] but the Chinese man will tell you, 'this law, you must review it'. You can start negotiation from morning to night with the Chinese man, you will never achieve one single thing. [...] The difficult employer is the Chinese man.

What has done even more to create negative perceptions of Chinese manufacturers in Nigeria are reports of serious health and safety failings and industrial accidents in Chinese-owned factories. The most notorious of these remains the fatal fire that occurred in 2002 at a large Hong Kong Chinese-owned factory in Ikorodu. Some initial estimates put the death toll at over 100 local workers, with later reports settling at a figure of around thirty (Akoni 2002; WSWS 2002). What was particularly shocking about this incident was the claim that most of the victims had perished because they had been locked inside by the management and were unable to escape (Ibharuneafe 2002b; WSWS 2002). These rumours had apparently spread even as the fire was taking hold, prompting locals to descend on the complex to vent their anger (WSWS 2002). While the full report of the Lagos state inquiry into the tragedy appears not to have been made public, this accusation against the Chinese management has persisted and continues to generate anger to this day (*Nigerian Compass* 2012; Oyesola 2010). Consequently, the incident is regularly cited as evidence of a particular association between Chinese companies and the maltreatment of local workers (*Business Day* 2011; CDWRN 2007; Oyeranti et al. 2011). As an Ikorodu resident who helped us to locate the factory, which does not welcome visitors and is still guarded by armed police, exclaimed upon our arrival: 'I don't like the Chinese, they have just come here to exploit us.'

These tensions between Chinese and African manufacturers and traders, or between Chinese employers and African employees, reflect competition within the same sectors or are part of a much wider process of class-based capitalist accumulation. Clearly, race, ethnicity and other social differences play into this political economy but we also found tensions between African employers and Chinese migrant workers where the questions of identity and local politics become even more important.

Contrary to most studies of Chinese and African labour relations which focus on Chinese employers (e.g. Giese 2013), we also found a number of Chinese workers employed in African-owned firms (see also Esteban 2010). Some of these are understandable in terms of specific skills, particularly in catering. Take the example of Mr Charles, a Ghanaian partner in a Chinese restaurant. He had seen that Chinese food was popular in Ghana so he thought he would start a Chinese restaurant serving genuine Chinese cuisine. He entered a partnership with a Chinese businessman and poached the chef from an existing restaurant in Accra. This story of West Africans initiating and managing Chinese restaurants was not uncommon. As a Hong Kong Chinese manager of a Chinese restaurant in Lagos said:

> There's a lot of Nigerian. You know they establish Chinese food and then they go to the restaurants, any restaurant, they try and link to contact the cook whether he can come and then he pay you like this you know, either the managers. [... Golden Dragon], it's very famous, it's owned by Nigerian, they employ manager and cook from main China.

In these cases there is a need for specialist skills. Other African business people who had hired Chinese workers debated their relative merits. The discussion was polarized between those who found Chinese workers more productive and skilled, and those who found local workers comparatively better. The middle ground, probably closest to the truth, was that you get good and bad workers in any system and there was no general pattern along national or racial lines.

Typical of those African entrepreneurs who lauded the industriousness of Chinese workers was a Nigerian urban development consultant from Lagos. He described the relative merits of Chinese workers:

> [The Chinese] were skilled people [...] We have them here but they are more expensive and they don't have the kind of quality of work that the Chinese were able to do, I tell you that [...] the quality we found in Nigeria was so terrible and it costs us three times [...] Now the Chinese man that you see in pushing the wheelbarrow and sweeping the floor is probably a mason then he is told to do that job and he is willing to do it. A Nigerian who is a mason will tell you that: No, he is a mason and he is not going to sweep.

Not only did issues of cost and productivity play into his calculations but there was also an issue of demarcation of roles, with the Chinese, according to this respondent, more willing to do menial jobs outside their ascribed skills set. Such positive sentiments about the Chinese work ethic were echoed by other African employers and were a recurrent theme in the attitude survey.

In contrast, some noted that Chinese workers were not inherently better. According to the general manager of a Ghanaian plant hire firm:

> [I]t is not all the Chinese guys that are hard-working as well, some have come here just to loaf around. So you also have to be on them to separate those who are hard-working and those who are not hard-working and at the same time our people as well some are receptive while some are resentful, we don't need these guys we know all that we need so you need to strike a balance.

While the rationale for bringing in relatively skilled workers to get the job done caused some anger, we found the most tension in cases where unskilled Chinese workers were brought in. One such case arose in Nigeria during our fieldwork in 2010. What angered Nigerians was that some major Nigerian companies were employing Chinese workers rather than locals, giving foreigners low- and semi-skilled jobs that most of Nigeria's unemployed masses could readily do.

In September 2010, a protest march was organized by the Lagos-based NGO Shelter Watch Initiative with support from the well-respected Campaign for Democracy and a number of trade unions, most notably the Nigeria National Fitters Association. The main targets of the protest were the French-owned company Lafarge Cement WAPCO Nigeria Plc and Nigeria's biggest indigenous conglomerate, the Dangote Group. On the placards and in the statements of those on the march, the former stood accused of employing 2,500 Chinese workers and the latter was chided for employing some 3,000 Chinese workers in the construction of its new cement factory in Ogun State (Okpi 2010).

Moreover, it was claimed that while the Dangote Group paid the relatively few locals employed in this construction project only NGN1,000 (c. £4) per day, it was paying the Chinese workers NGN8,000 per day. The Dangote Group attracted particularly strong criticism for this apparent favouring of Chinese over local workers not only because it proudly claims to be Nigeria's foremost indigenous commercial and industrial enterprise but also because its owner, Alhaji Aliko Dangote, is also the chairman of the Federal Government's National Committee on Job Creation. Indeed, the march culminated with a rally held outside the Lagos headquarters of the Group, at which demands were issued for Dangote to be removed from his chairmanship of the job creation committee and an attempt was made to deliver a letter calling for him to halt the employment of foreigners in jobs for which suitably skilled Nigerians are available. A trade unionist involved in organizing this protest exclaimed:

> It's painful. It's painful. Sometimes these people are not skilled men. They are helpers. In Nigeria we call them labourers. They are not skilled men [...] They send these people to Nigeria to go to their office, they are tea men, they are cleaners [...] These sort of people are taking money away. We are not against expatriate coming into the country to come and work. What we are saying at the same level, at the level of fitters, fabricators who can do the job you should employ them.

When we asked those behind the march why non-Chinese companies were apparently turning to foreign, principally Chinese, workers rather than locals, we were provided with a range of interesting theories. A popular theme was an elite conspiracy whereby the companies receive financial incentives, or other benefits such as privileged access to Chinese markets and technology, in return for taking on Chinese workers. A popular variation on this was that companies in Nigeria were receiving benefits from the Chinese state in return for employing Chinese convicts, furthering a Chinese policy to ease the pressure in China's supposedly overcrowded prisons. A senior figure in Shelter Watch noted:

> [W]hen you are bringing your prisoners, when you are bringing people, you are not going to fight with them, they are trampling on my rights. I am doing the job my brothers have to do, my brother don't have job – they are trampling on my rights.

Indeed, the notion that China is somehow trying to export its excess prisoners to Africa has gained considerable traction across the continent (see Hitchens 2008). However, even among the most ardent advocates of this theory that we met in Nigeria, the best supporting evidence advanced was that many of the Chinese workers in Nigeria *look* like convicts by virtue of wearing to work only simple 'slippers' (flip-flops) and dirty, torn 'rags' that appear as if they might once have been prison uniforms.

Despite the widespread public attention and debate excited by the issue of Chinese workers in Nigeria, it is significant that very little of the frustration appears to have been directed towards Chinese workers themselves. Indeed, as the protest against the Dangote Group suggests, most anger was directed at local business and political elites who have apparently encouraged Chinese workers to 'take' jobs that Nigerians can do. The channelling of anger towards local elites rather than Chinese workers is not simply part of the wider political economy of Nigeria, but is born out of a sense that these Chinese workers are in just the same position as most Nigerians; namely, forced to explore all options, including migration, in the daily struggle to make ends meet. While China's dramatic economic growth over the last twenty years has attracted much attention and no little admiration in Nigeria, there is also quite a widespread awareness that China is not now some kind of nirvana in which all are prosperous.

Conclusion

The arrival of Chinese employers, investors and workers has excited tensions in the African countries where they reside. In Ghana and Nigeria, as reported elsewhere in Africa, clear areas of tension and conflict have developed over the perceived threat to the personal safety of Chinese migrants, which has tended to see them remaining relatively isolated from their hosts. In terms of economic competition, we see relatively predictable lines of conflict where Chinese firms are operating more cheaply or more productively in sectors in which African entrepreneurs have had a sizeable presence. The respective states have made some attempt to intervene to regulate such activities but the general feeling on the part of local business people is that much more could be done to ensure 'fairer' competition. Within firms we see even more complex relationships with tensions between Chinese employers and African employees, though much of this is part and parcel of the accumulation process and not inherently about ethno-national differences between 'the Chinese' and 'the Africans'. That said, there are areas where cultural misunderstanding and prejudice play into this, resulting in negative, racialized stereotyping on both sides and even in the potential for violence. But the Chinese presence has not become anywhere near as politicized as in the much-emphasized Zambian case.

In the case of Nigeria, we saw that the employment of unskilled Chinese workers by leading Nigerian firms was the cause of much anguish, though all firms using Chinese labour defend their position on the grounds of the relative merits of Chinese workers over their local counterparts. This politicization of the Chinese presence was notable because the focus was not on the Chinese workers for 'flooding' the labour market but on the political and economic elites who encouraged it, or at least did not sanction it. This echoes Lee's (2009) work on African trade union responses to Chinese investment, where much of the protest and frustration was heaped on the African political elites who were allegedly in cahoots with Chinese elites. In Ghana, the recent debates about illegal Chinese gold mining have revealed a differentiation made on the part of Ghanaians between the 'good' aspects of China's presence – such as the big infrastructure projects – and the 'bad' elements such as the illegal migrants operating in these marginal and environmentally damaging sectors. The response in Ghana has been to deport the miners and make a public show of them while collaborating with their Chinese counterparts in the embassy. As yet the tensions have not become overtly politicized or racialized, though such potential is there. Moreover, many Ghanaians and Nigerians actively welcome the Chinese migrants, so the tensions detailed in this chapter can be understood in more nuanced ways than a simple 'Africans versus Chinese' analysis. Furthermore, Sino-African relations can also be much more convivial and mutually beneficial.

6 | BUILDING BRIDGES: TOWARDS CONVIVIALITY, COOPERATION AND MUTUAL BENEFIT IN SINO-AFRICAN ENCOUNTERS

Introduction

In the last chapter we examined the tensions that emerge from the presence of Chinese migrants in Africa. While much of the public commentary on this tension has focused on questions of labour and unfair competition (Giese 2013), we showed that the reasons for such tension are more diverse than this and that African actors are not absent from processes that ostensibly point the finger at 'the Chinese'. In this chapter we qualify some of the seemingly bald perceptions and accusations spoken by our respondents, and in some cases show the reverse; namely, that many of the relationships are amicable and productive.

As we noted in the last chapter, much of the underlying theory that critiques notions of 'Confucian capitalism' and posits the intersectionality of multiple axes of social difference are relevant to the discussions in this chapter and so are not repeated. In seeking to understand the everyday encounters across difference in the African societies we have been studying, we have added a discussion in the next section on conviviality and cosmopolitanism before analysing three areas where this conviviality is found. These three areas mirror the sites of tension in the previous chapter: understanding the pressures facing Africans and engaging with their cultures; the responses to Chinese trading and manufacturing enterprises; and more supportive relations within enterprises.

Conviviality in context

In terms of understanding processes of mixing and cross-cultural engagement, the concept of cosmopolitanism can help our analysis.

That said, much of the literature on cosmopolitanism is not only highly normative but implicitly deals with the West as the locus of cosmopolitan societies and/or as the source region for cosmopolitan sensibilities. Following Gidwani (2006) we want to 'provincialize' Europe and examine the cosmopolitanism of 'southern' sites. First, there is a long history of southern cosmopolitanism and encounter that links back to the histories we explored earlier. Considering the colonial metropolis, King writes:

> The first globally multi-racial, multi-cultural, multi-continental societies on any substantial scale were in the periphery, not the core. They were constructed under the very specific economic, political and social and cultural conditions of colonialism and they were largely, if not entirely, products of the specific social and spatial conditions of colonial cities. (King 1991: 8)

These hybrid social spaces were largely forged in the colonial period and King's caveat of 'specific conditions' is important since we have to be wary of naively celebrating these multicultural spaces that were shaped by hierarchies and power relations of various sorts. The point of seeing these complex societies in geographical and historical context is to emphasize their ordinariness. As Keith (2005) argues, we need a global sense of urbanism and multiculturalism as opposed to thinking of these terms as applying only to western contexts. Lagos, Accra, Tema and Kano are all cosmopolitan in their own way and this chapter is about exploring that simultaneous similarity and difference.

In seeking to hang on to what is similar and what is different, Knowles (2007) argues for a distinction between the cosmopolitan and cosmopolitanism, the former being a person with certain sensibilities and the latter a philosophical agenda. Most work focuses on the latter and forgets about the former, but this is possibly where our work lies – how do migrants and host societies interact? We have tried to think about this interaction in terms of conviviality, which is part of Gilroy's 'non-toxic' cosmopolitanism. Gilroy (1987) posits conviviality against those forms of normative cosmopolitanism. For him it is about the daily, lived multiculture of UK cities.

Overing and Passes (2000) concur that conviviality is about the sociality of societies and the agency of their members. They argue that modernist accounts of society and agency lack a sense of affect and so they use 'conviviality' to embrace this sense of affect and emotion in their studies of Amazonian societies. In terms of, say, work this is more about 'The congenial, convivial relations of work [that] are essential to a sociality that allows for very little coercive force, and no discord, with respect to the matter of work' (p. 16). However, Overing and Passes are not peddling some pristine utopia since convivial sociality carries within it the threat of destruction and the ending of social unity. So, the focus is on friendship, care, compassion and so on, but also on how the perceived or actual threat to tranquillity plays into the sense of sociality. Central to this, as the King quote implies, is the importance of place. Places shape the identities of the people in them, but this is not a local identity set against an abstract, and philosophically superior, notion of humanity. Rather, it is about how intersecting global and local relations are temporarily fixed in places and how these places in turn function as sites for slight and everyday, or sometimes deeper, encounters with difference (Amin 2002).

Destabilizing the divide: nuancing accounts of tension, conflict and difference in Sino-African encounters

'You need to adapt yourself into the new environment': putting the challenges of local society in perspective As we saw in the last chapter, Chinese respondents often see their African 'host' societies as presenting challenges that can make it difficult to settle and succeed, most notably crime, corruption and a less than dynamic labour force. While these narratives can render Africans and African societies as frustrating, hostile and even dangerous, the respondents also tend to qualify the extent of these problems and highlight how they can be accommodated through negotiation. What tends to be stressed here is both the importance of being able to adapt to the 'host' environment and a realization that local society can be easier to engage with than initial impressions suggest.

While there are widespread concerns about armed robbery, it

tends to be seen as a general problem rather than a specifically 'anti-Chinese' phenomenon. Furthermore, it is widely asserted that such crime is committed by only a very small minority of locals, is far from unique to the 'host' society and can be mitigated by the adoption of particular strategies. Exemplifying this more relaxed assessment of the threat, an established Lagos-based Chinese entrepreneur, who has been robbed in the city, even suggested that the potential dangers of such crime may be lower than elsewhere in the world:

> There are armed robbers all over the world [...] But the difference is that in Nigeria, the armed robbers don't kill you, they just steal your stuff. [...] You just have to be able to know how to take care of your own security, your personal security. [...] At night, you limit your going out [...] When you are going out you don't have to put all the gold in the world on your body, you don't have to show your money [...] If you just wear a tee shirt and a pair of shorts, you know, you are just like the normal average Nigerian person, nobody will touch you. And of course he will be very friendly with you, that's the difference! (Interpreter's translation from Chinese)

Some of the more established Chinese respondents also saw the problem of official harassment and corruption as a less daunting challenge than it first appeared, especially for their co-nationals who have uncertain legal status and/or limited proficiency in English. While the latter are often seen to be too quick to concede to demands for illicit payments when confronted by officials, the more established respondents contend that having a solid legal footing and the confidence and linguistic skills to argue one's case make it possible to resist such demands. There is also some recognition that these demands can be rather speculative and not as threatening as they seem. As a long-established Hong Kong Chinese manufacturer based in Kano reflected: 'Even in Lagos you see like the police chap, they just greeting you if they want something from you, but it is up to you, they won't force you.'

Where it is considered difficult or unwise to avoid the demands of local officials, such as in the case of securing the necessary permits to undertake particular economic activities, this generally appears to be accepted as a necessary and not especially onerous cost of doing business. 'I would say that's normal now,' said a Chinese shop manager in Accra, 'because if you are going to do something, get something done, you have to just slide over some money' (Interpreter's translation from Chinese). Moreover, as has been demonstrated elsewhere in Africa and beyond (Dobler 2008; Nyíri 2011), a pervasive system of petty corruption can provide an opportunity to develop mutually beneficial relationships with local officials. '[Y]ou have to identify those who can be useful to you,' argued another Accra-based Chinese shop manager, 'and if it means you have to spend some money to them for them to get what you want and to pave a way for you, we do that, that's life' (Interpreter's translation from Chinese). Developing such relationships can of course be useful for those who might wish to circumvent local regulations. Indeed, it was widely suggested in Nigeria that the large-scale importation of contraband textiles by local and Chinese traders was facilitated by regular payments to the authorities charged with imposing the ban (see also Axelsson 2012 in the case of Ghana).

For many Chinese entrepreneurs and managers, one of the most important areas of adaptation has involved the employment of local workers. As the previous chapter showed, there are widespread complaints by Chinese respondents that local employees are unproductive and difficult to work with. However, Chinese employers often assert that they have been able to devise ways to adapt to this challenge, while some contend that the challenge is not as great, or as culturally embedded, as many of their co-ethnics believe. The most basic adaptation to the perceived difficulties of working with locals is the development of tolerance. One of the most successful Chinese entrepreneurs in Accra, who arrived with a state-owned enterprise in the early 1990s and has gone on to establish a large importation, manufacturing and construction business employing some 400 locals, argued that one simply has to accept that Ghanaian workers are not always as productive as their Chinese counterparts and that projects can therefore take longer to complete than they would in China. Similarly, a Chinese respondent working for his family's import-export business in Accra, which employs around eighteen Ghanaians, asserted that it is important to be forgiving of minor human failings in local employees, especially when they have provided years of service. Referring to the five or six local members of staff who have been with the company since it started in the mid-2000s, he said:

[I]f they do something wrong, maybe sometimes you know the people need money, so maybe they thief something, but if it is not very serious we say, 'OK, let's forgive them' because we don't want make him to trouble because you know everybody is human being, we want [to] understand each other.

This respondent was also keen to point out that not all local staff are prone to committing such misdemeanours, adding: '[I]t depends, some be like this. You cannot say, "Oh, all of these people like this, all that people like this", cannot say it, it depends one by one.'

A reciprocal sense of understanding was found in a few responses in the attitude survey. We have noted that some Africans are aware of the relatively poor backgrounds of Chinese migrants, especially by the way they dress. A Ghanaian teacher in Takoradi noted:

Most of them come from a very poor background, so they would want to work very hard when given the opportunity so that they can meet the needs of their families back home. [...] They also have a tradition of making sure that they contribute their quota to the country, so I will say that they have the spirit of nationalism.

The empathy shown for the hardship they suffer and the dedication they show as a result is linked to a wider sense of national obligation, which the same respondent claimed was lacking among Ghanaians who are too self-centred.

Some Chinese employers appear to be more proactive in adapting to the perceived challenges of working with local staff. A key tactic here is to modify working practices imported from China to better suit what are understood to be the peculiarities of the local context. The Hong Kong Chinese owner of a Lagos-based construction company argued that in working with local employees, it was important to 'understand their culture. [...] It's not that you bring your own culture

[if] you want them to work with you together,' he continued, 'that one is not possible.' The Chinese manager of a modest, Chinese-owned assembly plant in Lagos, which was established in 2002 and employs sixty Nigerians, provided an example of how such a realization can be the basis for a process of negotiation with local workers:

> [I]n the western society, also in Nigerian society, every workers, they have right to strike, this one is different from China. So we also meet many times the workers strike for their rights. They ask us increase their salary for them. Now we already change many thing for them, we have to listen to the country, we have to listen to Nigeria. So before in China, the workers can work six days one week, one day they can work eight hours. But now we change it in Nigeria, our workers work maybe five to six hours one day, and five days for one week. Before we don't know how to manage [...] Now we talk with them, negotiate with them, we give them incentive and they will do their work by themselves and they are happy to finish their work.

In addition to altering working arrangements in response to the demands of local workers, this manager also realized that it was not possible to impose conditions of payment considered acceptable in China:

> [S]ometimes we['re] short of raw material, we will have to stop producing. If we no produce, we still pay the basic salary to the workers every month. [...] This one is better than in China. In China, we can delay one month salary [...] but not here.

Indeed, some Chinese employers found that if they offer relatively decent remuneration, local workers can be productive and easier to manage, with any cultural difference becoming less problematic. For example, a long-established Hong Kong Chinese manufacturer in Kano who tries to pay 'higher money' found that he has few problems with his 500 local employees and that they are 'quite good workers' and 'very good follower[s]'. He argued that proper payment is key to motivating workers whatever their cultural identity. 'So all the employees actually are the same,' he said. '[W]hether they are

Chinese or not Chinese [...] if I don't pay them money tomorrow, they will just run away!' This is often considered to be a priority in the case of especially valued local workers, with skilled, hard-working and/or long-serving local employees offered wage increases, promotions and rewards.

In attempting to build effective working relationships with local employees, the provision of training is also seen as important. Employing 200 Nigerians across his assembly plant in Lagos and his food-processing business in Kano, a Taiwanese entrepreneur with over twenty years' experience of operating in Nigeria said of local labour: '[I]f you are training them very well, let them know how to work, let them know what you want [...] they will work for you, completely.' Underpinning such assertions is often a sense that even when perceived deficiencies in the skills and attitudes of local labour are culturally embedded, they are nevertheless amenable to improvement. A Chinese entrepreneur who employs more than fifty Nigerians in his Lagos-based furniture factory, which he established in 2006, asserted: '[W]hen you talk about workers nobody is born bad. It is their environment that makes them bad. And of course nobody is born with the ability to do work so you have to train the person' (Interpreter's translation from Chinese). To support this contention, he pointed to the example of the Chinese people themselves, who, he believes, in addition to their experience of the Cultural Revolution, learned to work hard and progress through the investment of western companies in China. Reflecting Chinese state and public discourses framing recent migrants from China as new harbingers of global modernity (Nyíri 2006), he argued that Chinese enterprises are now involved in a similar process of foreign investment, instigating cultural change and greater productivity in Nigeria:

> [W]e believe that if we teach [Nigerians] how to work [...] they will
> be aware of time and how to work better, [...] already [...] there
> have been improvement in some of our staff here, we have taught
> them what hard work is all about and they appreciate it and they
> have improved.

Such sentiments have been taken on board by many of our African respondents. A regular refrain was that the Chinese work very hard and that this is something 'we' Africans should learn from. Talking of the lessons he has taken from the Chinese fishing crews he had seen, a Ghanaian harbour manager noted:

> Yes a lot of lesson. Like I said if we all remain focus, if there is something and all hands on deck we all do it. [...] Sometimes the Ghanaians working with them think that they are been pressurize because they don't have the excuse to say I am going to toilet and hide somewhere and smoke relax and come like Ghanaians do. They are always on it and when they have not finish they don't leave; even eaten I have not seen them.

An Accra-based Ghanaian importer who has done business with Chinese wholesalers in China also praised the Chinese work organization:

> Out in China they respect their workers and the workers work diligently because they take good care of them. I know they are fed three times a day and because of that they work very hard [...] If you go to a Chinese shop you cannot distinguish a boss from a labourer.

He notes the flatter hierarchy and the better treatment of the labour force – three meals a day – as something very different to Ghanaian business practice. Such views are at odds with the wider perception of the Chinese as particularly harsh employers, though the issue of discipline runs through both views.

By combining effective training with higher wages, the long-established Taiwanese entrepreneur quoted above believes that he has been particularly successful in developing a productive local workforce. While he believes his commitment to training and remuneration has been central to this, he downplayed any suggestion that Nigerian workers are especially in need of incentives and improvement, arguing that all workers are motivated by a desire to 'feed their family' and improve their 'life condition'. This is indicative of how some Chinese employers question negative stereotypes of local workers and provide more positive assessments, even making favourable comparisons with Chinese labour. For example, a Lagos-based Chinese entrepreneur described Nigerians as 'honest and hardworking' while a Chinese shop manager in Accra claimed: 'I trust Ghanaians more than Chinese. Ghanaians can work loyally for you.' In representations such as these, local labour does not appear to present the particular or profound challenges identified in the narratives of many Chinese employers. It is through processes of accommodation, negotiation and adaptation such as this that Chinese migrants have been able to settle and progress in Africa. As a Chinese shop manager in Accra said: '[Y]ou have to accustomize [sic] to the environment [...] You just get used to it, then you can get survival.'

'It's difficult to be anti-Chinese': the complexity of African responses to the Chinese 'threat' Just as the Chinese migrants engaged in this study often felt that their 'host' societies were not as hostile and challenging as they first appeared, African respondents tended not to see the increased Chinese presence only as a 'threat'. While the activities of Chinese enterprises have caused some notable resentment against 'the Chinese', we found that responses are much more complex than this. Even African respondents who felt they had been negatively affected often emphasized that the Chinese presence was not the sole cause of their problems and they did not necessarily engage in specifically 'anti-Chinese' agitation. In many cases, other foreign actors or even fellow locals were seen to be equally or even more responsible, with issues of local governance consistently highlighted as the most pressing problem. Indeed, rather than Chinese migrants or foreigners per se, it is overwhelmingly the state that is the target of resentment (see also Bourdarias 2010). Furthermore, negative reactions to the Chinese presence are often qualified and even countered by those who directly benefit from Chinese activities or believe there are positive social and economic outcomes.

These more complex responses can be seen in relation to the activities of Chinese traders and the treatment of local workers in Chinese enterprises. The Ghana Union of Traders' Associations' (GUTA's) agitation against Chinese traders in central Accra and beyond is part of a wider agitation against foreign traders in general. At GUTA's 2007 protest rally against 'the invasion of the retail trade by foreigners', it was not only Chinese traders who were pinpointed but also traders from India, Nigeria and Turkey (GNA 2007a). And while Chinese traders are widely considered to be prominent among these groups and have therefore attracted particular attention, it is Nigerian traders in Ghana that are seen to be the greatest cause of concern. Nigerian shops appear to have been particularly affected by Ghana Investment Promotion Centre clampdowns on foreign traders, prompting vocal complaints from Nigerian traders, politicians and officials (see, e.g., Ameyaw 2007; Ezugwu 2012). Indeed, the situation appears to have become even more politicized than the issue of Chinese traders, with reports of GUTA members directly harassing Nigerian traders and reprisals against Ghanaian traders in Nigeria (Ameyaw 2007).

Furthermore, it is widely recognized even among those who have expressed concern about the influx of 'cheap' Chinese products that it is local rather than Chinese traders who are primarily responsible. For example, the chief executive officer of one of Ghana's leading indigenous industries has, in his own words, 'been making a lot of noise' about cheap, low-quality imports from China undermining his business, but asserted:

China is actually not exporting into Ghana per se. Yeah, they make it available, [but] it's Ghanaians and Nigerians that go to China to order what they want to buy. They go, they see the dregs, they see the trash, they see the Rolls-Royces and what do they buy? Trash. That's what's coming here, it's not the Chinese fault [...] what the Ghanaian guys are doing, they are bringing these things in regardless of quality because they look at the money [i.e. cost]. [...] So I don't blame the Chinese [...] I blame the guys who go get that kind of stuff. [...] So it's difficult to be anti-Chinese.

Similarly, while the Manufacturers Association of Nigeria (MAN) has led agitation against the China Town in Lagos, one of its officials is clear that local traders are the main culprits in the importation of low-quality Chinese goods. '[A]ll these products are being based by specification, it's what the importers went there to request that they are giving to them,' he argued. This realization resulted in MAN focusing on local traders, joining with government in 'campaigning to change the orientation of Nigerians who go [to China] to make specification for lower-quality products'.

What is more, some local actors see the expanded presence of Chinese traders as having a positive impact and are prepared to defend their activities to some extent. There is considerable sympathy for the argument that the entry of Chinese traders has lowered the price local consumers pay for Chinese goods, and that this has a wider social benefit (see also Carling and Haugen 2008). For example, while a member of staff at the Kano Chamber of Commerce would prefer Chinese entrepreneurs to invest in the Nigerian textile industry, she nevertheless contended:

> [E]ven in the textile importation of clothes, I don't see much wrong because they have been able to clothe almost everybody, anybody can afford to get to them according to his capacity. We've had Vlisco brand from pre-independence up to now, not everyone can afford it. But the Chinese have come in and within a few years they've managed to clothe everybody.

A Ghanaian member of the Ghana–China Friendship Association, which is concerned with promoting Ghanaian products in China, agreed that Chinese traders have benefited local consumers by reducing the cost of Chinese goods. He argued that those making a 'big noise about the Chinese taking over the economy' are Ghanaian importers who previously enjoyed excessive profits on Chinese goods, 'so the Chinese themselves have come to give us the proper prices, so that is why they are not happy'. Notably, the Ghana Central Shopkeepers' Association, which is allied with GUTA, complained that local distributors, in the form of what are popularly known as 'market women', prefer to buy from Chinese traders and have even challenged GUTA's campaign against the Chinese presence in the market. Similarly, local distributors and a consumer organization in Senegal have lauded Chinese traders for lowering the price and increasing the range of consumer goods available and have actively countered local importers' protests against the Chinese trading presence (Dittgen 2010; Scheld 2010; 2011).

In addition to support for Chinese traders from consumers and local distributors, government officials and some elements of the organized private sector have a relatively relaxed attitude to the Chinese trading presence. This attitude stems from the belief that, in a globalized age, international flows of goods, people and investment are inevitable and, if managed properly, ultimately desirable. For example, an official in Ghana's Ministry of Trade and Industry explained: 'The rise of China is a reality and we have to accept it. The Chinese will come whether we like it or not.' They key is, he argued, to be proactive and shape the nature of the 'cooperation'. This would, he claimed, 'remove some of the trivial problems that have come to be associated with the Chinese, like people saying they are doing retail trade'. Tellingly, he went on to argue that 'we live in a global world and there are no borders any more'. The implication appeared to be that Ghanaians should be more accepting of the Chinese trading presence, which he saw as an inevitable part of a wider set of relations he and the Ghanaian government as a whole are working to build with China.

Similarly, while a senior official at the Kano Chamber of Commerce believes that the entry of Chinese traders should be subject to government regulation, he emphasized that such flows are inherent to the modern world and produce positive outcomes. In making this argument, he appeals to a sense of global citizenship as well as the economic benefits of international investment:

> In a globalized environment, [to] which we are all claiming to belong, it is very, very difficult to say the Chinese should pack off and go. Because the Chinese are in India, they are in America, they are in other Western European countries. [...] So definitely, Chinese people, you cannot just take them as intruders, so to say, or people that are not welcome. [...I]n economics there is nothing like stopping A, B, C, D from participating in a business. No! We are all universal citizens. [...] If you are bringing money from any country to come and invest in Nigeria, it is in the interest of the Nigerian economy. So if the Chinese people are bringing their money to invest in Nigeria, it is very, very good.

Chinese entrepreneurial investment is especially welcomed in the manufacturing sector, as this is seen to have the potential to contribute to local development. Stressing Kano's long history of being a cosmopolitan city that welcomes 'all people to come and do business', a senior official at the Kano State Ministry of Commerce, Industry, Co-operatives and Tourism explained that the state government 'see[s] the recent influx of the Chinese as an opportunity, not a threat' and hoped that Chinese traders will, after familiarizing themselves with the local market, 'want to turn to manufacturing the goods here'. To this end, he argued, the state government has put in place a range of incentives.

However, while there is openness to Chinese entrepreneurial investment in manufacturing, reservations about the treatment of local workers in Chinese enterprises, especially factories, remain. Yet even these undeniably serious concerns are often expressed in ways that are much more nuanced than is sometimes suggested. While it is widely believed that low pay, casualization and poor health and safety standards are problems in many Chinese-owned factories, these problems are not necessarily seen as unique to them. Indeed, it is often suggested that while Chinese factories may be among the worst offenders, similarly poor conditions are to be found in other foreign- and locally-owned enterprises (see also Hairong and Sautman 2013 for a similar argument in the case of Zambia's mining sector). The problem therefore comes to be framed as a wider challenge to the national manufacturing scene.

For example, a senior official of the Nigeria Labour Congress (NLC) in Lagos insisted that the prevailing labour conditions in Chinese manufacturing companies are little worse than those in other foreign-owned industrial enterprises in Nigeria. 'Basically, whether you talk about the Chinese, the Lebanese and the Indians, they have the same kind of business attitude,' he argued. 'They try to cut cost, that's labour cost.' He made it clear that the NLC and its affiliated unions have no particular animosity towards Chinese manufacturers. When the NLC picketed a Hong Kong Chinese-owned factory in Lagos in 2002 over its use of casual workers, the action was part of a wider campaign against casualization by local and multinational manufacturers (Ibharuneafe 2002a; Onoshevwe 2003). Alongside the Chinese company, other targets of the NLC's agitation were Nigerian companies such as the Eleganza Group and well-known multinationals such as Cadbury's, Dunlop, Guinness and Unilever.

Furthermore, Chinese manufacturers in Nigeria attract respect and even praise for being among the most resilient in the country. For example, the director general of MAN argued:

> [We] appreciate their investments in Nigeria, they are still very committed to investing, they have confidence in our economy no matter the situation whether you have religious problem or Niger delta problem or political problem, they believe they can still [invest]. So as far as I am concerned, the Chinese have assisted also in developing Nigeria. [...] They have never wavered.

One of his colleagues estimated that Chinese industrialists are responsible for at least 60 per cent of the investment that has been made in the country's manufacturing sector. The latter reported that 'in all facets of industry we have Chinese dominating', and provided the example of the steel industry, pointing to five Chinese companies which are major players, including one which he believes to be the largest steel producer in West Africa.

Given the high rate of unemployment in Nigeria, the local jobs created by Chinese manufacturers are especially appreciated. For example, one of the two largest Hong Kong Chinese manufacturing conglomerates is noted by a number of Nigerian and Chinese respondents for employing around 7,000 locals in Kano, and some 20,000 Nigerians across the country. Significantly, such important contributions to employment have produced some tolerance of the poor pay and conditions associated with Chinese manufacturers. A senior official of the National Union of Chemical, Footwear, Rubber, Leather and Non-Metallic Products Employees (NUCFRLNMPE) in Kano, who is himself quick to praise Chinese manufacturers for creating employment, said that even local workers tend to accept the conditions in Chinese factories for want of more lucrative alternatives: 'Because of lack of job around, the workers will say "Oh, sorry sir, if they can pay us as they are saying, OK, no problem, let's take it like that. Hard bread is better than none.'" Clearly, suggestions that poor pay and conditions are not exclusive to Chinese companies, and that this represents one of the better livelihood opportunities available, are unlikely to provide much solace to those who have to endure them.

However, they do indicate that rather than a specific 'anti-Chinese' agitation, we are witnessing the reinforcement of wider concerns about the negative effects of globalization. Furthermore, as we will go on to discuss in the following section, African respondents also identify more positive outcomes associated with the Chinese presence, which suggest that there is more than simply unbridled exploitation and inter-cultural conflict at play.

Building bridges: towards conviviality, cooperation and mutual benefit

Convivial and cooperative Sino-African relations: from hospitable locals and benevolent bosses to colleagues, friends and partners Narratives of tension and conflict in Sino-African encounters are further disrupted by accounts that highlight more convivial and cooperative relations. From the perspective of Chinese respondents, while there are widespread concerns about crime and corruption, local society is overwhelmingly seen to be hospitable. For example, a Chinese doctor running a clinic in Accra said, 'Ghanaian people is very kind [...] they have big heart to receive people [...] coming in', while a Chinese hotel manager in Lagos asserted of Nigerians, 'I like the people [...] they are honest and they are very nice to the foreign people'. A Chinese restaurateur in Tema argued that Ghanaians are 'very friendly' and will greet you in the street, noting that she had not experienced such public courtesy in Guangzhou, where she lived and worked prior to moving to Ghana. For a Chinese shop manager in Accra, what is especially impressive is that these greetings are sometimes communicated in Chinese, with basic Chinese salutations such as '*ni hao*' having become more widely known among Ghanaians. In Kano, the Chinese manager of an electrical equipment outlet recalled how he enjoys receiving and responding to greetings in Hausa each morning.

Although there are suggestions that such acts of apparent kindness can be motivated by a desire to receive financial benefits in return, basic hospitality is still often seen to be at play. Indeed, Chinese respondents reported encounters with locals that they consider to have involved largely selfless acts of hospitality. For example, a Chinese student in Accra recalled a taxi driver who came to find her to return the bag she accidentally left in his taxi, while the Kano-based Chinese manager of an electrical equipment outlet recounted how a local man gave him and his wife a lift home when they got lost while out walking one evening. Similarly, the Chinese owner of a furniture company based just outside Lagos recalled that some local men who work alongside the road that leads to her workshop helped her to fix her car when it broke down; they have since come to be 'friends'.

This example is indicative of the experience of many Chinese respondents who believe they have developed relations with locals that involve some degree of friendship (see also Park 2010). While these relations often emerge from, and remain bound up in, instrumental concerns about business, they are also framed as involving affective aspects that exceed purely economic interests. Chinese respondents operating in the retail and hospitality sectors often regard their regular local customers as 'friends' and emphasize that building these deeper connections is not only good for business but also enriches their experience of living and working abroad. A Chinese shop manager in the Lagos China Town reported that it is through having 'fun' chatting to well-known local customers that she has learned to speak English well, while the Chinese manager of a factory outlet in Tema insisted that becoming 'friends' with local customers enabled him to 'enjoy being in Ghana'. Similarly, a Hong Kong Chinese restaurateur noted that there are many local families who have been coming to her restaurant in Accra ever since she took it over twenty years ago:

> I like my business work because I like to see different people. This is funny job. Every day come for different people. Some is always come, like friend. Always I joking them. [...E]very day I get people come to talk to me, you have come to give me business, also come to talk to me, oh, this one is very good, you know. You must enjoy your work and then [if you] enjoy your work, you can do it well.

In some cases, convivial relations with local customers can extend beyond the social and spatial confines of economic exchange, such as shops and restaurants. Illustrating this, a Chinese respondent described how two of his 'best Ghanaian friends' are not only among the most important customers of his import business but are also a key part of his social life in Ghana; he visits their homes, plays football with them at weekends and brings their children gifts from China. With their relationship having become 'closer and closer', they recently joined him on a month's visit to China and while they identified goods they wanted to ship to Ghana, the primary purpose was to 'just enjoy'. Indeed, he recalled that a highlight of the trip was taking them to his home town to meet his family. This meeting went so well that it had the added benefit of easing his mother's reservations about him living in Ghana.

Despite all the tensions associated with Sino-African employment relations, many Chinese employers and managers report that they have not only been able to find effective ways of working with local staff but have also developed convivial and enduring relationships with some of their local employees (see also Kernen 2010). Explaining how she has come to speak English with Nigerian intonation and expressions, the Chinese furniture company owner based near Lagos revealed that she spent a long time living with her local staff in a shared compound, where they cooked and ate together and she learned how to prepare Nigerian dishes. The Chinese manager of an electrical equipment outlet in Kano fondly recalled that in his first job in Nigeria he was able to 'mix' and establish 'friendship' with the local workers, whom he regarded as 'the same like brothers' and who would invite him to their social events. Similarly, the Lagos-based Chinese hotel manager mentioned previously argued that a key reason why she feels 'very comfortable' in Nigeria and has remained there since the late 1980s is the good relationship she enjoys with her local staff: 'We are like friends. [...] I take the workers like my sister and brothers. [...S]o many of this staff they follow me all more than ten years and until today are still working for me. We understand [each other] very well, so that's why I am in this country.'

From the perspective of African respondents, there is some recognition that not all Chinese bosses are bad employers, and some are considered to offer better pay, conditions and prospects than many of their Chinese and non-Chinese counterparts. For example, the Ghanaian assistant in a Chinese shop in Accra who, as noted in the preceding chapter, feels he is badly treated by his current Chinese manager warmly recalled his previous Chinese manager with whom he experienced a much more cordial and benevolent relationship: '[H]e likes me, you know, I talk to him [...] Crack some jokes, you know [...] Oh, that man, I prefer him a lot [...] Although he's not having the money, he just tell you, "Just take this, OK, to survive."' In the manufacturing sector, a report by the NLC found labour relations that were 'regarded as a model in the industry' in a well-known Chinese textile factory in Lagos State (Atomre et al. 2009: 352). Similarly, the NUCFRLNMPE representative in Kano praised a Hong Kong Chinese-owned manufacturing group in the city for being open to the union and 'doing better' than most of the city's industries to provide decent employment. The owner of this group was one of the Chinese manu-facturers who emphasized the importance of paying higher wages in order to encourage commitment and hard work.

Furthermore, while skilled and managerial positions in Chinese enterprises tend to be dominated by Chinese staff, in many cases locals have had the opportunity to attain some of these positions. Chinese bosses emphasize that this simply makes good business sense – not only does it reduce the cost of recruiting increasingly mobile and expensive expertise from China but local staff are also particularly helpful in understanding the local market, man-aging local workers and negotiating the demands of local officials. For example, in the Hong Kong Chinese manufacturing group in Kano noted for its decent conditions, the Chinese manager spoke admiringly of the three Nigerian technicians who have worked with the company for over a decade since being recruited straight after graduating from a local university. The manager was proud that the technicians had gradually taken over the responsibilities of their older Chinese counterparts and risen to senior positions. In one of the Chinese factories in Tema, the manager is a Ghanaian who has become the owner's closest and most trusted deputy, having worked for him since the company was founded some thirty years ago. He oversees the fifty-eight local staff and three Chinese technicians at the factory and regards the owner as 'a brother' who has helped him greatly over the years, especially by enabling him to educate his children and sending him to China for medical treatment.

With local staff attaining more senior positions in Chinese enterprises, Ghanaians and Nigerians have come to know Chinese people not only as bosses but also as colleagues, creating opportunities for the development of convivial relations. Golden Telecoms, one of the three major Chinese telecommunication companies that have entered the Nigerian market since the late 1990s, has explicitly pursued a strategy of recruiting a high proportion of local staff for the reasons outlined above. A former Nigerian staff member reported that there is a Nigerian to Chinese staff ratio of about 2:1 in the company's Lagos office, with many local staff in middle management positions. However, there are complaints that Chinese staff sometimes appear to be favoured and that, contrary to official policy, meetings are occasionally held largely in Chinese. Furthermore, there is some resentment that a free canteen is provided for the exclusive use of Chinese staff, a practice that one Nigerian staff member describes as 'almost racist'. Nevertheless, the consensus among Nigerian staff was that their working relationships with Chinese colleagues are generally good and often friendly. For example, another Nigerian staff member remarked that he had 'made a lot of Chinese friends' at the company, adding, 'We all go for lunch, [they] take me to Chinese restaurant for their food, I take them to Nigerian restaurant, then they eat Nigerian food!' Such convivial relations can extend beyond the office, with a Nigerian staff member showing us photos of her wedding where her Chinese colleagues appear in the group shots.

Similarly, when we visited the Lagos headquarters of a Chinese company that sells quarry machinery, we found a smart open-plan office staffed by what appeared to be a very happy and close team of two Chinese and two Nigerians. We learned that the four men all knew each other from China, the two Nigerians being among an increasing number of their compatriots who have studied and/or worked there in recent years. The Nigerians had joined the company during their time in China and early in 2009 one of them was sent with a Chinese colleague to establish a sales office in Nigeria. These two pioneers formed a strong bond, the Chinese colleague remarking of his Nigerian counterpart: 'We try our best to do our jobs and everything I did, he know and everything he did, I know. We help each other.' The four men are of similar age, speak each other's language and have clearly become good friends. One of the Nigerians exclaimed:

> You know, I love my Chinese. When they come in, two, three days they have mixed up with the society [...] They find it so interesting, you know, going around. Now like Robert, he doesn't want to go back again, he is like stuck here! He doesn't want to go back. [He says,] 'Wow, Nigeria, I love it' and he's even planning [on] bringing his girlfriend around and he will have a kind of permanent residence here. They love it, they love it!

More convivial inter-ethnic relations such as these can also form the basis for Sino-African business partnerships. While these do not appear to be common and can end acrimoniously, some entrepreneurs find them to be mutually beneficial modes of more formal economic cooperation. A Chinese entrepreneur in Kano described his Nigerian partner in their quarry and construction company as a 'very good man' and said: 'He trusts me and I also 100 per cent trust him.'

In the Lagos China Town, a joint Chinese-Nigerian trading enterprise has grown out of one of the few Sino-African marriages we identified, with a Chinese wife and her Nigerian husband operating a successful clothes shop together. Mr and Mrs David were introduced to each other by a mutual Chinese friend whom Mr David had once helped. Mr David, himself a local official, soon became a source of informal assistance to Mrs David and they went on to marry a few years later in 2006, working together to grow the small trading business Mrs David had started in one of the largest shops in China Town.

A Hong Kong Chinese entrepreneur in Kano, Mrs Lu, wanted to secure her new business selling beverages produced by a Lagos-based Chinese company by winning the exclusive distribution rights for northern Nigeria. However, she was only able to gather the funds to pay the fee for this when contributions were made by two of her

Nigerian associates, one a long-standing customer of her fashion business and the other a man she had known for five years from a casino they both frequented. In return for their investments, she made them partners in the business and has paid them generous returns, remaining deeply grateful for what she sees as their 'generosity'.

For Mrs Lu, an added benefit of this arrangement is that a close relative of one of the partners is a senior police officer. He not only helped Mrs Lu when a local landlord attempted to defraud her but has also enabled her to take business risks she might not have done without his support. 'I feel very secured,' she revealed, 'even I give credit in the market because all the people know in the back is the [police officer].' This illustrates how Chinese enterprises in Africa often rely on developing relationships with local patrons in order to survive and prosper, just as Nyíri (2011) has suggested is the case across the less developed world.

Respondents who have been closely associated with the Lagos China Town argue that it is only the support of an influential Nigerian politician, who first brought over the Chinese founder as a business partner, which has enabled the complex to remain open in the face of protests and crackdowns. It is also notable that the largest Hong Kong Chinese manufacturing groups in Nigeria have prominent local figures on their boards; Michel et al. (2009) have shown how the connections of some of the most successful Chinese entrepreneurs in the country can go as high as the presidency. Similarly, Haglund (2008) highlights the role of local political appointees being placed on the boards of Zambian-Chinese joint ventures, and Dobler (2009) details how forging connections and controlling access to local officials has enabled Chinese business elites to emerge in Namibia. As a Nigerian involved in the management of the Lagos China Town contended: '[Y]ou know the business community in Africa, before you thrive you need somebody who is well established, a citizen who has the wherewithal to guide you, protect you in terms of the law and [has] connections.'

From convivial and cooperative Sino-African relations to African opportunities Beyond creating opportunities to enjoy convivial and cooperative cross-cultural interactions, involvement with Chinese enterprises can also provide Africans with the chance to develop their capabilities and so advance their careers and pursue new business opportunities. Illustrating how Africans can utilize Sino-African encounters to develop their social capital in productive ways, one of the growing number of Nigerians who rent shops in the Lagos China Town reported that he has built his business interests on the back of contacts he made while working for Chinese enterprises. As an engineering student, Mr Joseph had developed an interest in Chinese technology and was keen to gain experience of working with it. A relative who worked at a local Hong Kong Chinese-owned factory helped him to secure a job there and this enabled him not only to develop his professional skills and experience but also to become 'friends' with some of his Chinese colleagues. One of these introduced him to a Chinese entrepreneur who wanted to begin trading in Nigeria with a view to establishing a manufacturing business. Mr Joseph helped him identify a market niche and then left the factory to work as the manager of the new enterprise, which was based in China Town. After a few years, the Chinese entrepreneur decided that local conditions were not conducive to establishing a factory and returned to China. But through this entrepreneur and the China Town complex, Mr Joseph had further developed his network of Chinese contacts in both Nigeria and China and took advantage of this to establish his own business importing Chinese goods. Today, Mr Joseph has one of the most popular shops in China Town and is also utilizing his network to pursue his long-standing ambition to mine minerals in south-east Nigeria for export to China, his contacts having introduced him to Chinese investors who are interested in supporting the project.

Working with Chinese enterprises can also support African business development through human capital formation, with some African employees utilizing the skills and experience they acquired in Chinese companies to advance their own economic interests. For example, a Chinese entrepreneur who established a small door factory in Lagos discussed the Nigerian workers he recruited and trained with the assistance of two experienced Chinese technicians:

[B]efore all the boys, they don't know how to do doors, now [...] some of them they have stopped working for us, they are doing their own business outside because they now, they even repairing doors or doing some simple doors, they can do by themselves. Now because, because they learned the skill from us, they are doing for themselves now.

Similarly, the Chinese director of a partially state-owned Chinese construction company in Accra argued that when local labourers get 'very skilled' through the on-the-job training provided by the company, they often leave to take higher-paid casual work in the private sector, with some establishing small contracting companies of their own. In both Accra and Lagos, it appears that local waiters and chefs in Chinese restaurants have been able to use their training and experience to take advantage of the increasing opportunities in the cities' expanding hospitality sectors. As the Hong Kong Chinese manager of a high-end Chinese restaurant in Lagos said:

[H]ere a lot of food and beverage business they establish, no matter is Chinese food or continental [European] or Indian food, right, there's a lot of restaurant, hotels that open. And they open, they will need a lot of experienced staff so they will say [to the local staff], 'How much do they pay you, I can pay you double of that', and bargain like that, you know, and then [the local staff] will [say], 'OK, bye-bye then'.

Indeed, at one of the newer Chinese restaurants established in Accra, we found that the Ghanaian entrepreneur who is the lead partner in the business had poached not only a Hong Kong Chinese chef but also a local head waiter from one of his established Hong Kong Chinese competitors.

In the technology sector, working for Golden Telecoms has enabled local staff to launch careers in Nigeria's rapidly growing telecoms industry and wider corporate sector. The intensive, often hands-on training and rapid promotion it offers are seen by current and former Nigerian staff to provide the skills and experience necessary to secure better-paid jobs with the company's American and European competitors. Some Nigerian Golden Telecoms staff have used the expertise they have developed at the company to go on to establish or augment dynamic new Nigerian companies both within and beyond the telecoms sector. For example, a Nigerian former Golden Telecoms senior staff member argued that the knowledge and experience he gained at the company enabled him to establish a telecoms engineering services firm in 2007. 'We started by saying that we will sell knowledge,' he recalled, 'and all this came from my last place of work [...] The Chinese trained me.' His company now has sizeable contracts not only with Golden Telecoms but also with most of the other big telecoms companies in Nigeria and employs more than 100 staff, many of whom he has trained by drawing on his Golden Telecoms expertise. Similarly, another Nigerian former Golden Telecoms senior staff member left the company to join one of Nigeria's major up-and-coming technology firms in 2009 and is now its chief operating officer; the firm has grown to employ nearly 200 people. He attributes his meteoric rise to what he learned at Golden Telecoms: 'I was well tutored on how to run operations and how to do so many things so the glory goes back to Golden Telecoms.' As Bräutigam (2003) has suggested in the case of auto-parts manufacturers in south-east Nigeria, it would appear that contact with Chinese businesses can enable African entrepreneurs not only to develop new skills and capabilities but also to establish spin-off ventures of their own.

Conclusion

This chapter has shown that narratives of tension and conflict surrounding the Chinese presence are generally much less pervasive than is commonly assumed. What are regarded by some local interests as negative impacts associated with the activities of Chinese migrant entrepreneurs are often seen to be the inevitable and not always entirely undesirable outcomes of globalization, and little different from the effects of investments made by local and other international actors. It is also apparent that the tensions that do emerge tend not to simply pit Chinese actors against African actors but rather to expose competing African interests (see also Axelsson and Sylvanus 2010; Dittgen 2010). For example, local traders who directly import goods from China, and who have led much of the agitation against Chinese traders, have come up against local traders and consumers who do not have such transnational capabilities and have come to appreciate Chinese traders as a cheap source of Chinese goods. Similarly, officials and politicians excited by developing diplomatic and economic relationships with China often seem less concerned about calls by various social actors, such as trade unions, to regulate some of the activities of Chinese investors (Baah et al. 2009). In such ways, responses to the Chinese presence appear to have as much to do with African politics as they do with the politics of Sino-African relations (Mohan and Lampert 2013).

Furthermore, we have seen that Sino-African encounters can extend beyond tension and conflict to involve more convivial relations. However, it is important not to idealize these convivial encounters as the positionality of local actors is again key. For example, while the most senior Nigerian manager in one of the Chinese factories in Lagos made it clear that he is on very friendly terms with his Chinese boss and believes him to be a kind and generous employer, it has been reported that local manual workers in the same factory are paid low wages, do not have contracts and have been discouraged from forming a union. Just as Appiah argues that cosmopolitanism can be the 'warm glow of imperialism' (cited in Knowles 2007: 6), there is a danger that apparently convivial relations can be the warm glow of exploitation which forces us to consider the class alliances involved in such relations.

Nevertheless, the development of more convivial Sino-African relations is an important channel through which at least some African actors are able to leverage significant benefits from the Chinese presence. It is also clear that local actors can at times exert meaningful resistance to aspects of the relationship that run contrary to their interests. While the encounters that result may be less convivial, they rarely become specifically 'anti-Chinese' or violent. And any attempts to whip up such sentiments would have to overcome both the nuanced way in which Sino-African encounters are widely understood and the more convivial, cooperative and mutually beneficial relations that appear to be more developed than is often assumed.

7 | CONCLUSION: EVERYDAY SINO-AFRICAN ENCOUNTERS AND THE POTENTIAL FOR AFRICAN DEVELOPMENT

Introduction

This book has been about the everyday experiences of the presence of Chinese migrants in parts of Africa. As such it is about *both* China *and* Africa. We wanted to go beyond the formal state-to-state relationships that have dominated discussions of China in Africa thus far. While such bilateral relations are significant for both Chinese and African development, we wanted to move away from bounded understandings of development as something occurring at a national scale. Rather, development is organized by and unfolds through a multi-layered set of actors so that by necessity we break down all-encompassing categories such as 'the Chinese', 'Africans' and, for that matter, 'development' itself.

Through our own, largely qualitative, research and that of others, we have disaggregated the types of Chinese actors engaging with Africa at the present time, and situated their experiences within a longer history of engagements between China and Africa, as well as between these continents and their respective 'outsides'. As a result, we have also charted a course between global political economy that reduces all things to a capitalist imperative on the one hand and accounts that emphasize some essential 'Chinese' or 'African' characteristics on the other. Using ideas from economic sociology, gender studies and postcolonialism, we refocused on the intersections of class, race and gender in the experiences of migration and responses to it. A key insight here is that African actors have driven and/or shaped much of the engagement by Chinese migrants, which goes against most accounts that assume that the power always and ultimately lies with China (Mohan and Lampert 2013). In this conclusion we outline the broad theoretical and thematic issues covered in the book and identify the highlights from our data that illuminate them. From there we identify emerging trends and gaps in the field and suggest a series of broad policy implications arising from our work.

Key themes and contribution

One thing that has been lacking in accounts of China in Africa has been explicit theorization of the new dynamics involved in this relationship. Given the relative novelty of the phenomenon of growing flows of investments, aid, trade and people, most studies from the mid-1990s up until the last two or three years have been descriptive. That is to say, they have charted the scale of these flows using existing data, carried out surveys to collect more fine-grained data, or outlined a case study or two of a particular project or programme of engagement. Hence, our starting point was to develop a theoretical framework for trying to make sense of Chinese migration flows to Africa and what they mean for African development. We outline the major building blocks of the framework here, and support them with the specific and most notable findings from our data.

Migration and transformation Using Castles' (2009) work, we wanted to emphasize mobility as constitutive of social transformation rather than some aberration that will, through the right sorts of intervention, die down as development proceeds. By seeing multiple forms of globalization co-existing, we wanted to examine the unfolding relationships across space and the way that 'friction', from Tsing's (2004) work, brings such processes into being in particular places.

Our starting point for this was Chapters 2 and 3, which examined the long histories of contact between the peoples of the African continent and China. We showed that the relationships go back hundreds of years and have generally focused on trade and diplomacy as opposed to conquest and war. That is not to say that these motives are altruistic and certainly during the Cold War China's engagements with Africa were very much part of its geopolitical strategy, despite all the talk of solidarity. This history is used by the Chinese state to legitimize its current dealings with Africa, by suggesting that, as in the past, its recent relations are mutually enriching. Under European colonization we saw orchestrated movements of indentured labour to the Indian Ocean islands, East and Southern Africa. While many labourers returned at the end of their contracts, not all movement was of contracted labour and these groups formed the first real Chinese settler populations. Their presence over four or five generations has shaped the countries where they settled and in turn influenced subsequent migration flows from China.

In terms of the contemporary migrants we studied in our fieldwork, the period from the late 1940s is key since the formation of the People's Republic of China and the movement of the nationalists to Taiwan have been important turning points for Chinese migration to Africa. One issue was that some industrialists fled Communist China via Hong Kong before moving to Africa in the late 1950s. These were the first substantial wave we found in West Africa. Taiwanese investors also came to South Africa and elsewhere during the Apartheid era when many in the international community treated both states unfavourably. Their shared 'pariah' status saw strategic linkages between them, especially in the 1980s. The Maoist period was also significant for the policy experiments that created separation and hardship. While we need to be careful of reading into this a teleological and cultural argument that all Chinese people living through this period became immune to suffering, our older respondents, and some of their offspring, did mention that they learned to 'eat bitterness' during this time. Coming to Africa for them was a wrench, but in some senses it was a lot easier than the great difficulties experienced under Mao.

A related issue came with the liberalization of the economy from the early 1980s. As regulations concerned with mobility within and migration from China eased, and pressures for new markets intensified, we saw both state-backed and independent migration to Africa. Unlike many western powers that had engaged with Africa, for better and generally for worse, for centuries the Chinese appeared to see the continent as an opportunity. A 'frontier' mentality and a willingness to pursue relatively low-profit opportunities underpin this move, and for the state-owned enterprises the deep pockets of the Chinese state massively reduced the risk of these investments.

That said, African states and individuals deliberately encouraged the Chinese so these movements to Africa over the past cannot be read as purely the outcomes of Chinese desires.

In terms of the organization and attitudes of these more recent Chinese arrivals, within a generation China moved from developing to, arguably, an upper-middle-income country, despite massive and growing inequalities. For those who sought their livelihoods overseas in Africa, the recent memory of being less developed played into their attitudes to work and lifestyle. At one level, as we saw in Chapters 5 and 6, the work ethic of Chinese migrants is generally celebrated and many Africans noted that they have far less hierarchical working practices. On the other hand, many Chinese in Africa felt that Africans were missing an opportunity because they lacked the discipline to get their economies going in the way that China had. We return to these debates over 'development' presently.

Embeddedness and Confucian capitalism Another issue we addressed was the question of the specificity versus generality of capitalist processes. One line of argument has stressed the specificity of a Chinese version of capitalism based on Confucian values and holds that when Chinese people 'travel' this model of doing business travels with them. In contrast, we argued for an entwining of capitalist processes across space, which produces combined and uneven development. Such an entwining is sensitive to the particularities of capitalist processes in specific places, but does not allow the 'cultural' determinants of this organization of the economy to blind us to the essential features of capitalism. In this way we have to maintain class as a central focus of our study as opposed to the ethno-cultural framing that has inflected so much scholarship on China-in-Africa to date. Indeed, through the idea of intersectionality we sought to include a bundle of social differences in any given explanation of tension or conviviality.

Chapter 4 examined the organization of Chinese business networks. It focused on those firms that were family based and noted that the gender relations within many were relatively egalitarian. We also found firms that were headed by women and/or in which it was women who had been the drivers of the decision to move to Africa. There was some use of family labour but increasingly competitive, arm's-length recruitment procedures were being used. We also found that the notions of an ethnic economy were overblown, with a great deal of competition and dissonance between firms. Overlaying this individualism was some sense of a shared associational life but by and large it was informal sociality that was most important for sub-groups of Chinese migrants. Within this, use of the internet was important for existing and would-be migrants. Contrary to the characterization of Chinese businesses as exploitative and enclaved, we found that most of the small and medium-sized enterprises had considerable engagement with the local economy. These firms acted as employers, suppliers, retailers and business partners. In these ways Chinese migrants came to know more Africans and vice versa.

Another rebuttal of the idea of Chinese firms as necessarily successful was evidence that many had struggled and failed. Discourses outside and within Africa suggest that the unfair practices of Chinese business people mean that they can only ever triumph, something bolstered by the 'Chinese capitalism' arguments, which are geared to explain the cultural underpinnings of success. Rarely do they discuss the negative aspects of business practices or the more mundane fact that many small businesses, wherever they are in the world, tend to fail. In this respect, Chinese firms in Africa are no different, though this is not to belittle the site-specific difficulties they face.

Mediation, conviviality and African agency While the preceding chapters tended to take a relatively Chinese-centred perspective, Chapters 5 and 6 sought to examine the more negative and positive aspects of the relationships between Chinese and Africans. Such relations are conditioned by the interplay of different axes of social difference and, as we noted, this has to be rooted in class, given that we are examining what are a group of business people seeking to extract profit of some sort. Playing into these social divisions are wider political discourses and institutional practices, all of which play out in specific ways in unique localities. So, while we used general notions of intersectionality and conviviality these can only be given meaning in specific contexts.

Chapter 5 examined the more 'tense' relations between some Chinese and some Africans. Such tensions have been emphasized in much of the reporting of China in Africa, and while we do not deny their existence we wanted to explore the multiple root causes of such tensions. One issue was a real and perceived threat from 'Africans' towards our Chinese respondents. This partly explained some Chinese migrants' enclave mentality and the practice of dealing with locals on a needs-only basis. We also examined sectoral tensions, which are possibly the easiest to understand, whereby African traders and manufacturers, in particular, felt threatened by Chinese small and medium-sized enterprises in these sectors. There were some attempts by business associations and trade unions to support African claims in this regard but by and large the enforcement of local laws was patchy, leading many to assume that there was an elite interest in not disciplining malpractice. When there had been an effort by the state to control competition and sanction Chinese business people, this was often tied to political capital, such as around election times.

From the sectoral tensions we moved within firms to examine employee–employer relationships and those between colleagues. Given that many Africans are employed by Chinese firms, it is imperative to focus on class processes even if the tensions are represented by the protagonists in racial and ethnic terms. Tensions arose over productivity and pay, with a sense on the Chinese employer side that 'Africans' were not very productive and for this reason did not deserve high wages. That said, many employers realized that better wages tended to secure more loyal and effective staff, which is not a revelation unique to cross-cultural employment relations. We also found some Chinese workers who were employed by African firms, which further complicates the relationship between class and race. Like their Chinese counterparts, African employers stressed the relative productivity of Chinese workers vis-à-vis their African employees, though such perceptions were not universal. Such employment practices in Nigeria had excited trade union action as it was seen as indefensible that low-skilled labourers should be brought in to do the work that the mass of Nigeria's un- or under-employed could do. Such conflicts speak to the transnationalization of class forces, since the decision to employ Chinese workers was based on logics of surplus extraction rather than loyalty to one's 'own'.

Chapter 6 mirrored these tensions by looking at the subtlety of some of the arguments surrounding these relationships as well as the explicit conviviality found across cultures. Again, some of this could be explained in class terms, though more in terms of class as cultural capital since friendships and business alliances tended to be between Chinese and Africans of similar status. Moreover, while the debate has focused on 'the Chinese' versus 'Africans', in many African discourses people pointed out that the Chinese were only doing what other outsiders have done and continue to do. Namely, 'the Chinese' are no worse although the fact that they are simply no worse than others who have exploited Africa is hardly a ringing endorsement of their activities. However, it does point to the fact that the Chinese presence is simply part and parcel of Africa's globalization, and not anything too exceptional. Despite these more nuanced takes on the role of China in Africa, we still found instances of friendships and mutual learning across the cultures with active agency on the part of many Africans to maximize the benefits from the Chinese. For example, African respondents used employment with Chinese firms to learn business practices and then set up their own firms; and African traders alerted Chinese businesses to the opportunities of African markets.

Emerging trends, gaps in our knowledge and policy implications

The preceding summary suggests that our knowledge of these complex migration flows is growing apace, as are those studies of African migrant communities in China. Here we identify some gaps in our knowledge, partly as a result of the boundaries of our own study, which inevitably meant some issues could not be addressed or only came to light as we conducted the research. But there are also gaps as a result of new trends in this rapidly changing field.

Our study of Chinese migrants in Africa has argued that they are an important social, economic and – potentially – political force in African development. But, as we noted in Chapter 3, the wider context for much of this inward migration is that Africa's strategic role has increased in the past decade. This is largely focused on the key mineral and energy resources found on the continent as well as the potential of its land and water resources. It is also a geopolitical issue involving security and fighting extremism, although the seriousness of these threats is sometimes used to justify the interventions designed to lock up the resources. Our study also showed that Africa is seen by some as a potential market. In the Chinese case we looked at the big infrastructure projects, which give Chinese state-owned enterprises construction contracts and a toehold in African markets. It is also about the small traders and manufacturers who sell the consumer and capital goods so badly needed in African economies.

The rise of some African economies, however, is not just about opportunities for China, though this has become the *cause célèbre* in policy circles and academic debate. Spurred on by their example and with the economies of the global North stagnating, western governments have begun to represent Africa as a new frontier in the quest for economic recovery, calling on entrepreneurs and businesses to put aside their old reservations and invest in the continent. Alongside this, there are reports that growing numbers of unemployed citizens from some of the most troubled European economies are now migrating to Africa in search of jobs and business opportunities, suggesting that it is also necessary to recognize the development of novel 'North–South' trajectories.

With these important new dynamics overlaying long-standing migration flows within and to Africa, there is a need to better understand the nature, activities and impacts of the expanding and more diverse expatriate communities that are being produced on the continent. While a nascent literature has begun to explore the growing Chinese presence in Africa, little is known about recent migrants arriving from other 'emerging powers' which are increasingly engaging with the continent, such as India and Brazil. Consequently, it is unclear to what extent the Chinese presence is exceptional or emblematic in terms of how migrants from emerging economies are engaging with Africa. Furthermore, there is little research on contemporary expatriate communities formed in Africa by migrants from the more established world powers, even though these often have a considerable history and appear to be gaining new impetus in the wake of the global economic crisis. And while there is greater recognition of the importance of the international migration of Africans within Africa, we still have a limited understanding of these flows and how they compare with those originating from beyond the continent.

In Chapter 5 we discussed the tensions between Chinese migrants and some elements of the African societies where they reside. We noted that this is largely a class-based issue sometimes expressed, rather worryingly, in ethnic and cultural terms. However, such demonizing of 'the Chinese' is not unique to African societies but is prevalent in many western discourses about China. Moreover, African political actors seeking to present themselves or their party as the true custodians of a nation's welfare have at times exaggerated the depth of this animosity. That said, these are very real concerns and should not be swept under the carpet. At one level our data suggest that once 'Chinese' and 'Africans' get to know one another better such tensions can dissipate. And those tensions between employer and employee are not so different from those found in many small businesses the world over. We should not belittle them but their structural roots in capitalist processes mean that they are unlikely to be transcended in the near future and are unlikely to spawn violent resistance, given the fragmentation of small firms.

Where the tensions are most worrying is at the sectoral level and where political elites are complicit in some way in the continuation of these practices. We are not arguing that Chinese business people are, by nature, prone to malpractice since our data showed that in some case it is weak regulation that allows for poor practice; indeed, some Chinese businesses operate in an exemplary fashion. But where impacts are felt within an entire sector and where political organizations can effect change then it is here we are likely to see the most vigorous resistance. Key sectors such as trading, construction, some manufacturing, fishing and other smaller-scale resource-extracting activities are likely to be where most tension is found as African livelihoods suffer.

Playing into these tensions, as our Nigerian case in particular showed, is a sense that state authorities are not concerned about the plight of impoverished Africans. Some interpret this as a concerted conspiracy theory between elites and argue that the Chinese must have 'bought off' key political players. Others are more sanguine and see this mode of governance as par for the course for their country – favouring selected external actors is nothing peculiar to the Chinese presence. In these cases the Chinese may be the targets for ire, but it is only in the context of an ongoing and grinding feeling that the rulers do not share the spoils of multinational capital, of whatever scale or origin.

Playing into this we are also likely to see a growing Chinese presence in domestic politics in Africa. While the Chinese state, for example, stresses 'non-interference', we have seen that this was always something of a myth and is now breaking down. If this proves to be the case then this has major implications for politics in these countries, as well as for relations between the rising powers and 'established' powers that have long held trusteeship over these states. Hence, we are likely to see growing direct involvement in African governance. This is likely to be below the radar rather than through public governance programmes, and the knowledge of African politics is growing through strategic individuals. However, as a Ghanaian local government worker in Takoradi commented in our attitude survey: 'If they do not get themselves involved in our politics, then one will admit that they have to stay with us even more but if they enter into our local politics then they will have problems with us.'

While much of this involvement will be led by Chinese state actors, other migrant communities in Africa, notably the Lebanese in West Africa and Indians in East Africa, have come to play more political roles. While we should not read off from history too rigidly, as Chinese entrepreneurs become more embedded in African economies their need to influence local policy will grow and our data show that some are entering such processes, albeit in very low-key ways.

This focus on governance and development opens up the final issue: what can be done to enhance the development benefits for Africa from what many agree will be a growing phenomenon? The preceding discussion suggests that, in fact, the Chinese are not so different from other external actors engaging in Africa and that tensions are most intense at the sectoral level and where political responses are deemed to be inadequate. When we asked respondents in our attitude survey what they felt could be done to enhance the gains from the Chinese presence, many pointed to China as some sort of model. When we asked if they felt China was more successful than African countries, 68 per cent of Ghanaian respondents and 45 per cent of Nigerian respondents agreed that China was. When asked why they thought this, many (around 40 per cent) pointed to China's technological superiority.

Some also noted that the Chinese 'understand' the development process in Africa better because they have only recently passed through that stage themselves. As a Ghanaian advertising agent in Accra noted of the Chinese:

> I think we need them now more than we need anybody. Why?
> Because they have been where we have been not too long ago, and
> irrespective of how much we like this, they are certainly going
> to be the single power in the whole world not too far from now.
> I think we are all in self-denial when we refuse to believe that. It
> will be better to have them on our side and have them interested
> in us than to have them against us.

Certainly this echoes the recognition of the realities, and indeed inevitabilities, of a globalized world that may look very different from the old order that dominated for much of the last century. That said, a new order, focused on Asia, will still be a capitalist one and so the possibilities for African development are likely to be constrained. But there is a sense that Africa has to embrace this globalization rather than fight it, something the African Renaissance in South Africa acknowledged over a decade ago.

Another set of answers in our survey of African attitudes related to what could be done to improve the benefits from Chinese investment in terms of local employment and local content. The following statements from two Ghanaian respondents in Takoradi, the first a teacher and the second an administrator, are exemplary:

If I were put in charge of affairs, before I award a contract to a Chinese man I will make sure that he agrees that if the contract is given to him he will employ Ghanaians to work on the project. If the Ghanaian is not given the administrative work to do they should at least be given the semi-skilled work to do, that is, they must be employed at levels where they can also help in decision-making and not always pushed around to do the donkey jobs.

I think we have to tighten up our immigration laws, and make sure that anybody who the law catches is dealt with severely without any favour. [...] I will not only deal with the Chinese alone but all foreigners in the country. I will make sure that they abide by the rules and regulation in the country.

Both responses speak directly to the questions of policy. The first states a clear need for local people to get employment in foreign ventures, although as they acknowledge this is not an issue unique to the Chinese. The second quote, in a refrain echoed repeatedly, raises the need for local enforcement of regulations concerned with immigration, wages, health and safety, and taxation.

These concerns echo recent calls by Ngozi Okonjo-Iweala, one of the then managing directors of the World Bank (Okonjo-Iweala 2010), setting out a clear agenda for leveraging more strategic benefits from China's engagement in the resource sector. She urged the Chinese to make investments consistent with national development priorities, which at root means creating jobs. Chinese firms should, she argued, also demonstrate transparency and operate legally and add value by locating more elements of the value chain in Africa. They should pay the taxes due and avoid bribery and engage the local communities. As we noted, it is not so much the lack of legal protection but the lack of its enforcement. Having said that, Ghana is currently debating a Local Content Law in Parliament, largely in response to the oil sector, though the issue of local jobs from inward investment clearly goes wider than this sector alone. Moreover, many of Okonjo-Iweala's recommendations relate to purposive industrial policy, which has been absent from African development plans since the start of the neo-liberal era.

Developing and implementing coherent industrial policy would appear particularly important given that a wide range of our African respondents, including government officials, private sector representatives, trade unions and workers, often stressed their desire for a stronger industrial sector and greater manufacturing employment. Significantly, these respondents tended to see this as the area in which Chinese investors could make their greatest contribution. Indeed, in Chapter 6 we noted that it was recognized that Chinese investors are already making substantial contributions to industrial employment in Ghana and Nigeria, with large, long-established Hong Kong Chinese conglomerates and a growing number of smaller Chinese-owned factories employing thousands of workers across the two countries. Concordantly, it is often manufacturing that Chinese entrepreneurs identify as the area of greatest investment potential in Africa and they tend to bemoan the fact that the barriers to realizing this are poor governance and infrastructure. If a stable and attractive policy environment could be established alongside infrastructural investment, they argue, significant manufacturing growth and economic development could be achieved. As a Lagos-based Chinese manufacturer asserted: 'I was even thinking Nigeria should be better because Nigeria land is rich. People, population is much. [...] If Nigeria government work like the Chinese, I am sure Nigeria will be like Singapore.'

But as we have argued in this book, realizing the potential of Chinese investment for African development relies not only on the formal, macro-level politics of government policy but also on the everyday, micro-politics of inter-cultural encounter and exchange. While so much coverage has focused on the tensions and conflicts involved in these Sino-African interactions, we have seen that they can also display real potential for producing more convivial, cooperative and mutually beneficial relations. Appropriate economic policies concerned with investment and industrialization could undoubtedly further such relations, but their development requires support through African social policy for migrant integration, local education and training, and the protection of local workers. Here African agency and the dynamics of African politics, both formal and every day, again become key in understanding China–Africa relations. It is in this interaction between the formal realm of politics and the informal spaces of social relations that the future developmental impacts of China in Africa will be determined.

BIBLIOGRAPHY

Ahiuma-Young, V. (2009) 'Chemical, leather workers petition minister over activities of Lee Group', *Vanguard*, 17 September.

Akinrinade, S. and O. Ogen (2008) 'Globalization and de-industrialization: South-South neo-liberalism and the collapse of the Nigerian textile industry', *The Global South*, 2(2): 159–70.

Akoni, O. (2002) 'Ikorodu fire: NLC rep faults Warp', *Vanguard*, 2 November.

Alden, C. (2005) 'China in Africa', *Survival*, 47(3): 147–64.

— (2007) *China in Africa*, London: Zed Books.

Alden, C. and M. Davies (2006) 'A profile of the operations of Chinese multinationals in Africa', *South African Journal of International Affairs*, 13(1) 83–96.

Ameyaw, D. (2007) 'Ghana: Nigerian traders want fair treatment', *Modern Ghana*, 4 December, www.modern ghana.com/news2/149116/1/nigerian-traders-want-fair-treatment.html (accessed 20 January 2014).

Amin, A. (2002) 'Ethnicity and the multicultural city: living with diversity', *Environment and Planning A*, 34: 959–80.

Ampiah, K. and S. Naidu (2008) 'The Sino African relationship', in K. Ampiah and S. Naidu (eds), *Crouching Tiger, Hidden Dragon: Africa and China*, Scottsville: University of KwaZulu-Natal Press.

Arnold, D. (2012) 'Spatial practices and border SEZs in Mekong Southeast Asia', *Geography Compass*, 6(12): 740–51.

Atomre, E., J. Odigie, J. Eustace and W. Onemolease (2009) 'Chinese investments in Nigeria', in A. Y. Baah and H. Jauch (eds), *Chinese Investments in Africa: A Labour Perspective*, Windhoek: African Labour Research Network.

Axelsson, L. (2012) *Making Borders: Engaging the Threat of Chinese Textiles in Ghana*, Stockholm: Acta Universitatis Stockholmiensis.

Axelsson, L. and N. Sylvanus (2010) 'Navigating Chinese textile networks: women traders in Accra and Lomé', in F. Cheru and C. Obi (eds), *The Rise of China and India in Africa: Challenges, Opportunities and Critical Interventions*, London: Zed Books, pp. 132–41.

Ayers, A. (2012) 'Beyond myths, lies and stereotypes: the political economy of a "new scramble for Africa"', *New Political Economy*, 18(2): 227–57, www.tandfonline.com/doi/abs/10.1080/13 563467.2012.678821 (accessed 1 June 2012).

Baah, A. Y. and H. Jauch (eds) (2009) *Chinese Investments in Africa: A Labour Perspective*, Windhoek: African Labour Research Network.

Baah, A. Y., K. N. Otoo and E. F. Ampratwurm (2009) 'Chinese investments in Ghana', in A. Y. Baah and H. Jauch (eds), *Chinese Investments in Africa: A Labour Perspective*, Windhoek: African Labour Research Network.

Babalola, L. and A. Lawal (2002) 'Labour Congress rallies against casual

workers syndrome – pickets Wahum',
P.M. News, 8 April.

Bailey, P. (2012) *Women and Gender in Twentieth-Century China*, Basingstoke: Palgrave Macmillan.

Ballard, R. (2012) 'Geographies of development: without the poor', *Progress in Human Geography*, 36(5): 562–71.

Bank of China (2011) 'Bank of China launched "Chinese Desk" in Ghana', www.boc.cn/en/bocinfo/bi1/201104/t20110418_1360045.html (accessed 28 November 2013).

Barabantseva, E. (2005) 'Transnationalising Chineseness: overseas Chinese policies of the PRC's central government', *Asian*, 96: 7–28.

Bayart, J. (2000) 'Africa in the world: a history of extraversion', *African Affairs*, 99(395): 217–67.

BBC (2012) 'Nigeria accuses Chinese traders of "scavenging" in Kano', 22 May, www.bbc.co.uk/news/world-africa-18169983 (accessed 25 May 2013).

Beckman, B. (1982) 'Whose state? State and capitalist development in Nigeria', *Review of African Political Economy*, 23: 37–52.

Berger, P. (1987) 'An East Asian developmental model?' in P. Berger and M. Hsiao (eds) (1988) *In Search of an East Asian Development Model*, New Brunswick: Transaction Books, pp. 3–11.

Bergesen, A. (2008) 'The new surgical colonialism: China, Africa, and oil', paper presented at the American Sociological Association Annual Meeting, Boston, MA, 31 July 31.

Biao, X. (2003) 'Emigration from China: a sending country perspective', *International Migration*, 41(3): 21–48.

Bodomo, A. B. (2010) 'The African trading community in Guangzhou: an emerging bridge for Africa–China relations', *China Quarterly*, 203: 693–707.

Bonnett, A. (2010) 'Radicalism, anti-racism and nostalgia: the burden of loss in the search for convivial culture', *Environment and Planning A*, 42(10): 2351–69.

Bourdarias, F. (2010) 'Chinese migrants and society in Mali: local constructions of globalization', *African and Asian Studies*, 9: 269–85.

Bourdieu, P. (1986) 'The forms of capital', in J. G. Richardson (ed.), *Handbook of Theory and Research for the Sociology of Education*, New York: Greenwood, pp. 241–58.

BP (British Petroleum) (2011) *BP Statistical Review of World Energy 2011*, London: BP.

Bräutigam, D. (1998) *Chinese Aid and African Development: Exporting Green Revolution*, Basingstoke: Macmillan.

— (2003) 'Close encounters: Chinese business networks as Industrial catalysts in sub-Saharan Africa', *African Affairs*, 102(408): 447–67.

Bräutigam, D. and X. Tang (2011) 'African Shenzhen: China's special economic zones in Africa', *Journal of Modern African Studies*, 49(1): 27–54.

Bredeloup, S. (2012) 'African trading post in Guangzhou: emergent or recurrent commercial form?', *African Diaspora*, 5(1): 27–50.

Broadman, H. (2007) *Africa's Silk Road: China and India's New Economics Frontier*, Washington, DC: World Bank.

Brooks, A. (2010) 'Spinning and weaving discontent: labour relations and the production of meaning at Zambia-China Mulungushi textiles', *Journal of Southern African Studies*, 36(1): 113–32.

Bürkner, H.-J. (2012) 'Intersectionality: how gender studies might inspire the analysis of social inequality among migrants', *Population Space Place*, 18: 181–95.

Bush, R., J. Bujra and G. Littlejohn (2011)

'The accumulation of dispossession', *Review of African Political Economy*, 38(128): 187–92.

Business Day (2011) Editorial, 'Asian companies and human rights abuse', 9 March.

CAITEC (Chinese Academy of International Trade and Economic Cooperation) (2010) 'China–Africa Trade and Economic Relationship Annual Report 2010', www.focac.org/eng/zxxx/t832788.htm (accessed 28 November 2013).

Carling, J. and H. Ø. Haugen (2008) 'Mixed fates of a popular minority: Chinese migrants in Cape Verde', in C. Alden, D. Large and R. Soares de Oliviera (eds), *China Returns to Africa: A Rising Power and a Continent Embrace*, London: Hurst, pp. 319–38.

Carmody, P. (2011) *The New Scramble for Africa*, Cambridge: Polity Press.

Carmody, P., G. Hampwaye and E. Sakala (2012) 'Globalisation and the rise of the State? Chinese geogovernance in Zambia', *New Political Economy*, 17(2): 209–29.

Castles, S. (2009) 'Development and migration – migration and development. What comes first? Global perspective and African experiences', *Theoria*, 56(121): 1–131.

— (2010) 'Understanding global migration: a social transformation perspective', *Journal of Ethnic and Migration Studies*, 36(10): 1565–86.

— (2012) 'Cosmopolitanism and freedom? Lessons of the global economic crisis', *Ethnic and Racial Studies*, 35(11): 1843–52.

CDWRN (2007) 'Chinese firms' "dehumanising" treatment of Nigerian workers', Campaign for Democratic and Workers' Rights in Nigeria, 25 February, www.nigeriasolidarity.org/art047.htm (accessed 2 December 2012).

Chalfin, B. (2008) 'Cars, the customs service, and sumptuary rule in neoliberal Ghana', *Comparative Studies in Society and History*, 50(2): 424–53.

Chang, D., M. Farooki and H. Johnson (2013) 'Culture, livelihoods and making a living', in T. Papaioannou and M. Butcher (eds), *International Development in a Changing World*, London: Bloomsbury Academic.

Chang, I. (2003) *The Chinese in America: A Narrative History*, New York: Penguin Group.

Chang, J. and J. Halliday (2005) *Mao: The Unknown Story*, London: Jonathan Cape.

Chang, S. (1968) 'The distribution and occupation of overseas Chinese', *Geographical Review*, 58(1): 89–107.

Chen, Y. (2012) 'FDI by overseas Chinese to dip', *Global Times*, 24 August, http://english.peopledaily.com.cn/90778/7923395.html (accessed 28 November 2013).

Chidaushe, M. (2007) 'China's grand re-entrance into Africa – mirage or oasis?', in M. Manji and S. Marks (eds), *African Perspectives on China and Africa*, Cape Town, Nairobi and Oxford: Fahamu, pp. 107–18.

Colombant, N. (2006) 'West Africa attracts influx of Chinese entrepreneurs', *Voice of America News*, 19 May, www.voanews.com/content/a-13-2006-05-19-voa52/398955.html (accessed 28 November 2013).

Corkin, L. (2013) *Uncovering African Agency: Angola's Management of China's Credit Lines*, Farnham: Ashgate.

Crawford, D. (2000) 'Chinese capitalism: cultures, the Southeast Asian region and economic globalisation', *Third World Quarterly*, 21(1): 69–86.

Daily Independent (2006) 'MAN wants owners of sealed shopping malls prosecuted', 11 January.

Das, R. J. (2012) 'From labour geography to class geography: reasserting the Marxist theory of class', *Human Geography*, 5(1): 19–35.

Davies, M., H. Edinger, N. Tay and S. Naidu (2008) *How China Delivers Development Assistance to Africa*, Stellenbosch: South Africa: Centre for Chinese Studies, University of Stellenbosch.

Davis, K. (2008) 'Intersectionality as buzzword: a sociology of science perspective on what makes a feminist theory successful', *Feminist Theory*, 9: 67–85.

De Haan, A. (1999) *Social Exclusion: Towards an Holistic Understanding of Deprivation*, London: Department for International Development.

Dikkoter, F. (1992) *The Discourse of Race in Modern China*, Stanford, CA: Stanford University Press.

Ding, S. (2007) 'Digital diaspora and national image building: a new perspective on Chinese Diaspora Study in the age of China's rise', *Pacific Affairs*, 80(4): 627–48.

Dirlik, A. (1997) 'Critical reflections on "Chinese capitalism" as paradigm', *Identities*, 3(3): 303–30.

Dittgen, R. (2010) 'From isolation to integration? A study of Chinese retailers in Dakar', Occasional Paper, 57, China in Africa Project, Johannesburg: South African Institute of International Affairs.

Dobler, G. (2005) *South-South Business Relations in Practice: Chinese Merchants in Oshikango, Namibia*, unpublished paper.

— (2008) 'Solidarity, xenophobia and the regulation of Chinese businesses in Namibia', in C. Alden, D. Large and R. S. de Oliveira (eds), *China Returns to Africa: A Rising Power and a Continent Embrace*, London: Hurst, pp. 237–55.

— (2009) 'Chinese shops and the formation of a Chinese expatriate community in Namibia', *The China Quarterly*, 199: 707–27.

Downs, E. S. (2007) 'The fact and fiction of Sino-African energy relations', *China Security*, 3: 42–68.

Dunning, J. H. and S. M. Lundan (2008) *Multinational Enterprises and the Global Economy*: Cheltenham: Edward Elgar.

ECOWAS-SWAC/OECD (2006) *Atlas on Regional Integration in West Africa*, www.oecd.org/swac/publications/38409391.pdf (accessed 28 November 2013).

Ellis, R. (2011) 'The politics of the middle: re-centring class in the postcolonial', *ACME*, 10(1): 69–81.

Ernst and Young (2012) *Building Bridges: Ernst and Young's African Attractiveness Survey 2012*, www.ey.com/ZA/en/Issues/Business-environment/2012-Africa-attractiveness-survey (accessed 17 January 2014).

Esteban, M. (2010) 'A silent invasion? African views on the growing Chinese presence in Africa: the case of Equatorial Guinea', *African and Asian Studies*, 9: 232–51.

Ezugwu, A. (2012) '2,000 Nigerian businessmen in Ghana may return home', *Newswatch*, 22 July.

Fairbank, J. K. and M. Goldman (1992) *China: A New History*, Cambridge, MA: Belknap Press/Harvard University Press.

Ferguson, J. (2006) *Global Shadows: Africa in the Neoliberal World Order*, Durham, NC: Duke University Press.

Fessehaie, J. and M. Morris (2013) 'Value chain dynamics of Chinese copper mining in Zambia: enclave or linkage development?', *European Journal of Development Research*, 25: 537–56.

Findlay, A. and F. Li (1999) 'Methodologi-

cal issues in researching migration',
Professional Geographer, 51(1): 50–9.

Foster, V., W. Butterfield, C. Chuan and
N. Pushak (2009) *Building Bridges:
China's Growing Role as Infrastructure
Financier for Sub-Saharan Africa*,
Washington, DC: World Bank.

France Diplomatie (2008) www.
diplomatie. gouv.fr/fr (accessed
5 January 2014).

Fraser, A. and J. Lungu (2007) *For Whom
the Windfalls? Winners and Losers in
the Privatisation of Zambia's Copper
Mines*, Lusaka: Civil Society Trade
Network of Zambia, Lusaka, www.
sarpn.org/documents/d0002403/1-
Zambia_copper-mines_Lungu_Fraser.
pdf (accessed 29 September 2011).

French, H. and L. Polgreen (2007)
'Chinese flocking in numbers to a new
frontier: Africa', *International Herald
Tribune*, 17 August, www.iht.com/
articles/2007/08/17/news/malawi.
php (accessed 19 January 2014).

Gadzala, A. (2009) 'Survival of the
fittest? Kenya's *jua kali* and Chinese
businesses', *Journal of Eastern African
Studies*, 3(2): 202–20.

Geschiere, P. and F. Nyamnjoh (2000)
'Capitalism and autochthony: the
seesaw of mobility and belonging',
Public Culture, 12(2): 423–52.

Gibson-Graham, J. K. (2006) *A Post-
capitalist Politics*, Minneapolis, MS:
University of Minnesota Press.

Gidwani, V. K. (2006), 'Subaltern cosmopolitanism as politics', *Antipode*,
38(7): 21.

Giese, K. (2013) 'Same-same but different:
Chinese traders' perspectives on African Labor', *China Journal*, 69: 134–53.

Giese, K. and A. Thiel (2012) 'The vulnerable other – distorted equity in
Chinese Ghanaian employment relations', *Ethnic and Racial Studies*, DOI:
10.1080/01419870.2012.681676.

Gilroy, P. (1987) *There ain't No Black in
the Union Jack: The Cultural Politics
of Race and Nation*, London: Unwin
Hyman.

— (2004) *After Empire*, London: Routledge.

GNA (2005) 'Ghana's investment law to
be reviewed', *Ghana News Agency*,
14 July.

— (2007a) 'Government urged to enforce Investment Code', *Ghana News
Agency*, 14 November.

— (2007b) 'Shops protest foreign
invasion of retail trade', *Ghana News
Agency*, 14 November.

— (2010) 'Foreign traders asked to
abide rules', *Ghana News Agency*,
30 March.

Granovetter, M. (1985) 'Economic action
and social structure: the problem of
embeddedness', *American Journal of
Sociology*, 91(3): 481–510.

— (1995) 'The economic sociology of
firms and entrepreneurs', in A. Portes
(ed.), *The Economic Sociology of
Immigration: Essays on Networks,
Ethnicity and Entrepreneurship*, New
York: Russell Sage Foundation,
pp. 128–65.

Gray, J. (2010) *Rebellions and Revolutions:
China from the 1800s to 2000*, New
York: Oxford University Press.

Greenhalgh, S. (1994) 'De-orientalizing
the Chinese family firm', *American
Ethnologist*, 21(4): 742–71.

Gu, J. (2009) 'China's private enterprises
in Africa and the implications for
African development', *European Journal of Development Research Special
Issue on China, India and Africa*, 24(1):
570–87.

— (2010) 'China's private enterprises in
Africa and the implications for Afri-
can development', paper presented
at the ESRC Rising Powers Workshop
'China and Low Income Countries:
Actors, Modes of Interaction, and
Analytical Innovations', School of

Oriental and African Studies, University of London, 23–24 September.

Haglund, D. (2008) 'Regulating FDI in weak African states: a case study of Chinese copper mining in Zambia', *Journal of Modern African Studies*, 46(4): 5487–575

— (2009) 'In it for the long term? Governance and learning among Chinese investors in Zambia's copper sector', *The China Quarterly*, 199: 627–46.

Hairong, Y. and B. Sautman (2010) 'Chinese farms in Zambia: from socialist to "agro-imperialist" engagement?', *African and Asian Studies*, 9: 307–33.

— (2013) '"The beginning of a world empire"? Contesting the discourse of Chinese copper Mining in Zambia', *Modern China*, 39: 131–64.

Harris, K. L. and J. Pieke (1998) 'Integration or segregation: the Dutch and South African Chinese compared', in E. Sinn (ed.), *The Last Half Century of Chinese Overseas*, Hong Kong: Hong Kong University Press.

Hart, G. (1996) 'Global connections: the rise and fall of Taiwanese production network on the South African periphery', Working Paper 6, California: University of California, Institute of International Studies.

Harvey, D. (2003) *The New Imperialism*, Oxford: Oxford University Press.

Hattingh, D., B. Russo, A. Sun-Basorun and A. Wamelen (2012) *The Rise of the African Consumer*, Johannesburg, South Africa: Mckinsey and Company.

Haugen, H. Ø. (2011) 'Chinese exports to Africa: competition, complementarity and cooperation between micro-level actors', *Forum for Development Studies*, 38(2): 157–76.

Haugen, H. Ø. and J. Carling (2005) 'On the edge of the Chinese diaspora: the surge of Baihuo business in an African city', *Ethnic and Racial Studies*, 28(4): 639–62.

He, M. B. (2009) *Overseas Chinese Journal of Bagui*, http://bbs.tianya.cn/post-worldlook-265686–1.shtml (accessed 28 November 2013).

Heimer, M. and S. Thogersen (eds) (2006) *Doing Fieldwork in China*, Copenhagen, Denmark: NIAS Press.

Henderson, J. (2008) 'China and global development: towards a global Asian era?' *Contemporary Politics*, 14(4): 375–92.

Hirsch, E. (2013) 'Ghana deports thousands in crackdown on illegal Chinese goldminers', *Guardian*, 15 July, www.theguardian.com/world/2013/jul/15/ghana-deports-chinese-goldminers (accessed 25 November 2013).

Hitchens, P. (2008) 'How China has created a new slave empire in Africa', *Daily Mail*, 28 September, www.dailymail.co.uk/news/worldnews/article-1063198/PETER-HITCHENS-How-China-created-new-slave-empire-Africa.html (accessed 5 February 2011).

Ho, C. (2008) 'The "doing" and "undoing" of community: Chinese networks in Ghana', *China Aktuell*, 3: 45–76.

Holslag, J. (2011) 'China and the coups: coping with political instability in Africa', *African Affairs*, 110(440): 367–86.

Hoogvelt, A. (1997) *Globalisation and the Postcolonial World: The New Political Economy of Development*, London: Macmillan.

Hsu, E. (2002) '"The medicine from China has rapid effects": Chinese medicine patients in Tanzania', *Anthropology and Medicines*, Special Issue, 9(3): 291–314.

— (2007) 'Zanzibar and its Chinese communities', *Populations, Space and Place*, 13(2): 113–24.

Huang, W. and Wilkes, A. (2011) 'Analysis of China's overseas investment policies', CIFOR Working Paper 79, www.cifor.org/publications/pdf_files/WPapers/WP-79CIFOR.pdf (accessed 28 November 2013).

Huang, Y. (2007) 'A comparative study of China's foreign aid', *Contemporary International Relations*, 17(3): 81–93.

Human Rights Watch (2011) *'You'll be Fired if You Refuse': Labor Abuses in Zambia's Chinese State-owned Copper Mines'*, New York: Human Rights Watch.

Huynh, T. T. (2008) 'From demand for Asiatic labor to importation of indentured Chinese labor: race identity in the recruitment of unskilled labor for South Africa's gold mining industry, 1903–1910', *Journal of Chinese Overseas*, 4(1): 51–68.

Huynh, T. T., Y. J. Park and A. Y. Chen (2010) 'Faces of China: new Chinese migrants in South Africa, 1980s to present', *African and Asian Studies*, 9: 286–306.

Ibharuneafe, S. (2002a) 'NLC President's war', *Newswatch*, 20 May.

— (2002b) 'Factory goes up in flames, killing 15 workers in Ikorodu', *Newswatch*, 30 September.

Jacques, M. (2009) *When China Rules the World: The Rise of the Middle Kingdom and the End of the Western World*, London: Allen Lane.

Jazeel, T. (2011) 'Spatializing difference beyond Cosmopolitanism: rethinking planetary futures', *Theory, Culture & Society*, 28(5): 75–97.

Kahn, H. (1979) *World Economic Development: 1970 and Beyond*, New York: Morrow Quill.

Kaplinsky, R. and M. Morris (2006) 'Dangling by a thread: how sharp are the Chinese scissors?', http://oro.open.ac.uk/8584/ (accessed 28 November 2013).

Karugia, J. N. (2010) 'The Chinese in Tanzania: migrants and investors', *Duke East Asia Nexus*, 2(1): 6–16, http://issuu.com/duke.nexus/docs/dean_2.1 (accessed 28 November 2013).

Keith, M. (2005) *After the Cosmopolitan? Multicultural Cities and the Future of Racism*, London and New York: Routledge.

Kernen, A. (2010) 'Small and medium-sized Chinese businesses in Mali and Senegal', *African and Asian Studies*, 9: 252–68.

King, A. (1991) 'Introduction: spaces of culture, spaces of knowledge', in A. King (ed.), *Culture, Globalization and the World-System*, Basingstoke: Macmillan, pp. 1–18.

Kirshner, J. (2012) '"We are Gauteng people" challenging the politics of xenophobia in Khutsong, South Africa', *Antipode*, 44: 1307–28.

Klutse, F. D. and E. Ennin (2007) 'Shops close in Accra', *Daily Guide*, 16 November.

Knowles, S. (2007) 'Macrocosmopolitanism? Gilroy, Appiah, and Bhabha: the unsettling generality of cosmopolitan ideas', *Postcolonial Text*, 3(4): 1–11.

Kopinski, D., A. Polus and I. Taylor (2012) 'Contextualising Chinese engagement in Africa', in D. Kopinski, A. Polus and I. Taylor (eds), *China's Rise in Africa: Perspectives on a Developing Connection*, London: Routledge, pp. 1–8.

Kragelund, P. (2008) 'The return of non-DAC donors to Africa: new prospects for African development?', *Development Policy Review*, 26(5): 555–84.

— (2010) *The Potential Role of Non-traditional Donors' Aid in Africa*, ICTSD Programme on Competitiveness and Sustainable Development, Issue Paper 11, Geneva, Switzerland: International Centre for Trade and Sustainable Development.

Kuah-Pearce, K. E. (ed.) (2004) *Chinese Women and Their Cultural and Network Capitals*, Singapore: Marshall Cavendish International.

Lancaster, C. (2007) *The Chinese Aid System*, Center for Global Development, www.cgdev.org/content/publications/detail/13953/ (accessed 28 November 2013).

Large, D. (2009) 'China's Sudan engagement: changing northern and southern political trajectories in peace and war', *The China Quarterly*, 199: 610–26.

Laribee, R. (2008) 'The China shop phenomenon: trade supply within the Chinese diaspora in South Africa', *Afrika Spectrum*, 43(3): 353–70.

Larkin, B. D. (1971) *China and Africa, 1949–1970: The Foreign Policy of the People's Republic of China*, Berkeley, CA and London: University of California Press.

Lawson, V. and the Middle Class Poverty Politics Research Group (2012) 'De-centring poverty studies: middle-class alliances and the social construction of poverty', *Singapore Journal of Tropical Geography*, 33(1): 1–19.

Lee, C. (2009) 'Raw encounters: Chinese managers, African workers and the politics of casualization in Africa's Chinese enclaves', *The China Quarterly*, 199: 647–66.

Lee, M. (2007) 'Uganda and China: unleashing the power of the dragon', in H. Melber (ed.), *China in Africa*, Uppsala: Nordiska Afrikainstitutet.

Lentz, C. and P. Nugent (eds) (2000) *Ethnicity in Ghana: The Limits of Invention*, Basingstoke: Palgrave.

Levitt, P. and R. de la Dehesa (2003) 'Transnational migration and the redefinition of the state: variations and explanations', *Ethnic and Racial Studies*, 26(4): 587–611.

Li, A. (2000) *A History of Chinese Overseas in Africa*, Beijing: Chinese Overseas Publishing House.

— (2012) *A History of Chinese Overseas in Africa to 1911*, New York: Diasporic Africa Press.

Li, H.-F. (2001) 'Exile of the Chiang K'ai-shek regime to Taiwan', www.twhistory.org.tw/20011210.htm (accessed 28 November 2013).

Lincoln, D. (2006) 'Beyond the plantation: Mauritius in the global division of labour', *Journal of Modern African Studies*, 44(1): 59–78.

Live, Y. (2005) 'Reunion island', in L. Pan (ed.), *The Encyclopedia of the Chinese Overseas*, Singapore: Nanyang Technological University, pp. 356–9.

MacFarquhar, R. (1980) 'The post-Confucian Challenge', *The Economist*, 9(2): 67–72.

Manji, M. and S. Marks (eds) (2007) *African Perspectives on China and Africa*, Cape Town, Nairobi and Oxford: Fahamu.

March, G. P. (1996) *Eastern Destiny: Russia in Asia and the North Pacific*, Connecticut: Greenwood Publishing Group.

Marfaing, L. and A. Thiel (2011) 'Chinese commodity imports in Ghana and Senegal: demystifying Chinese business strength in urban West Africa', Working Paper 180, Hamburg: German Institute of Global and Area Studies.

Mathews, G. and Y. Yang (2012) 'How Africans pursue low-end globalization in Hong Kong and Mainland China', *Journal of Current Chinese Affairs*, 41(2): 95–120.

Mawdsley, E. (2008) 'Fu Manchu versus Dr Livingstone in the dark continent? Representing China, Africa and the West in British broadsheet newspapers', *Political Geography*, 27(5): 509–29.

Mayda, A. M. (2005) 'International

migration: a panel data analysis of economic and non-economic determinants', Discussion Papers 1590, Institute for the Study of Labor (IZA).

Mbachu, D. (2006) 'Nigerian resources: changing the playing field', *South African Journal of International Affairs*, 13(1): 77–82.

McCall, L. (2005) 'The complexity of intersectionality', *Signs*, 30(3): 1771–800.

McCaskie, T (2008) 'The United States, Ghana and oil: global and local perspectives', *African Affairs*, 107(428): 313–32.

McCord, E. A. (1993) *The Power of the Gun: The Emergence of Modern Chinese Warlordism*, Berkeley, CA: Cambridge University Press.

McKeown, A. (1999) 'Conceptualizing Chinese diasporas, 1842 to 1949', *Journal of Asian Studies*, 58(2): 327–30.

McKinsey Global Institute (2010) *Lions on the Move: The Progress and Potential of African Economies*, www.mckinsey.com/insights/mgi/research/productivity_competitiveness_and_growth/lions_on_the_move (accessed 28 November 2013).

— (2012) *The Rise of the African Consumer*, www.mckinsey.com/insights/consumer_and_retail/the_rise_of_the_african_consumer (accessed 17 January 2014).

McNamee, T. with G. Mills, S. Manoeli, M. Mulaudzi, S. Doran and E. Chen (2012) *Africa in Their Words: A Study of Chinese Traders in South Africa, Lesotho, Botswana, Zambia and Angola*, Discussion paper, Lesotho: Brenthurst Foundation, www.thebrenthurstfoundation.org/files/brenthurst_commisioned_reports/Brenthurst-paper-201203-Africa-in-their-Words-A-Study-of-Chinese-

Traders.pdf (accessed 25 November 2013).

Meagher, K. (2012) 'Weber meets Godzilla: social networks and the spirit of capitalism in East Asia and Africa', *Review of African Political Economy*, 39(132): 261–78.

Michel, S., M. Beuret and P. Woods (2009) *China Safari: On the Trail of Beijing's Expansion in Africa*, New York: Nation Books.

Mohan, G. (2013) 'Chinese migrants as agents of South–South cooperation', in J. Dargin (ed.), *The Rise of the Global South: Philosophical, Geopolitical and Economic Trends of the 21st Century*, Singapore: World Scientific.

Mohan, G. and B. Lampert (2013) 'Negotiating China: reinserting African agency into China–Africa relations', *African Affairs*, 112(446): 92–110.

Mohan, G. and M. Tan-Mullins (2009) 'Chinese migrants in Africa as new agents of development? An analytical framework', *European Journal of Development Research*, 21: 588–605.

Monson, J. (2009) *Africa's Freedom Railway: How a Chinese Development Project Changed Lives and Livelihoods in Tanzania*, Bloomington, IN: Indiana University Press.

— (2011) 'Railway time: technology transfer and the role of Chinese experts in the history of TAZARA', in T. Dietz (ed.), *African Engagements: Africa Negotiating an Emerging Multipolar World*, Leiden: Koninklijke Brill NV.

Moyo, D. (2009) *Dead Aid: Why Aid is Not Working and How There is a Better Way for Africa*, London: Allen Lane.

Mthembu-Salter, G. (2009) *Elephants, Ants and Superpowers: Nigeria's Relations with China*, Johannesburg: South African Institute of International Affairs.

Mudimbe, V. (1988) *The Invention of Africa: Gnosis, Philosophy, and the Order of Knowledge*, London: James Currey.

Mung, M. E. (2008) 'Chinese migration and China's foreign policy in Africa', *Journal of Overseas Chinese*, 4: 91–109.

Naim, M. (2007) 'Rogue aid', *Foreign Policy*, 159(March/April): 95–6.

Nash, J. (2008) 'Re-thinking intersectionality', *Feminist Review*, 89: 1–15.

Nation, The (2008) 'NLC reports LEE Group to NECA over alleged maltreatment of workers', *The Nation*, 18 August.

Ngome, I. (2009) 'Cameroonian perceptions of the Chinese invasion', *AfricaFiles*, www.africafiles.org/article.asp?ID=15986 (accessed 18 September 2011).

Nigerian Compass (2012) Editorial, 'Safety and health at work', *Nigerian Compass*, 27 April.

Nonini, D. and A. Ong (1997) 'Introduction: Chinese transnationalism as an alternative modernity', in A. Ong and D. Nonini (eds), *Ungrounded Empires: The Cultural Politics of Modern Chinese Transnationalism*, London: Routledge, pp. 3–33.

Nonor, D. (2009) 'GIPC sets up national task force ... to clamp down on illegal business activities', *The Chronicle*, 17 July.

Nyíri, P. (2006) 'The yellow man's burden: Chinese migrants on a civilizing mission', *China Journal*, 56: 83–106.

— (2011) 'Chinese entrepreneurs in poor countries: a transnational "middleman minority" and its futures', *Inter-Asia Cultural Studies*, 12(1): 145–53.

Obasola, K. (2006) 'China Town for made-in-Nigeria goods', *The Punch*, 11 April.

Obiorah, N. (2007) 'Who's afraid of China in Africa? Towards an African civil society perspective on China–Africa relations', in F. Manji and S. Marks (eds), *African Perspectives on China in Africa*, Oxford: Fahamu, pp. 35–56.

Ogidan, A. (2004) 'MAN seeks review of trade relations with China', *Guardian*, 28 July.

Okere, R. (2006) 'China Town: an aberration to Nigeria's industrial development plan, say manufacturers', *Guardian*, 18 January.

Okonjo-Iweala, N. (2010) 'Promoting smart and responsible investment in Africa', *All Africa*, www.worldbank.org/en/news/speech/2010/11/15/promoting-smart-responsible-investment-africa (accessed 19 January 2014).

Okpi, A. (2010) 'Go back to your country', *Next on Sunday*, 26 September.

Ong, A. (2002) 'Flexible citizenship among Chinese cosmopolitans', in J. Vincent (ed.), *The Anthropology of Politics: A Reader in Ethnography, Theory and Critique*, Oxford: Blackwell, pp. 338–55.

Onoshevwe, R. (2003) 'NLC and the war against casualisation', *Daily Independent*, 18 June.

Overing, J. and A. Passes (eds) (2000) *Anthropology of Love and Anger: The Aesthetics of Conviviality in Native South America*, London: Routledge.

Oyeranti, G. A., M. A. Babatunde and E. O. Ogunkola (2011) 'An analysis of China–Nigeria investment relations', *Journal of Chinese Economic and Foreign Trade Studies*, 4(3): 183–99.

Oyesola, B. (2010) 'Safety at work: Nigerian workers, the endangered species', *NBF News*, 3 January, www.nigerianbestforum.com/blog/?p=72819 (accessed 4 December 2013).

Page, B. and C. Mercer (2012) 'Why do people do stuff?: Reconceptualizing remittance behaviour in diaspora-development research and policy', *Progress in Development Studies*, 12(1): 1–18.

Pan, L. (ed.) (2005) *The Encyclopedia of the Chinese Overseas*, Singapore: Nanyang Technological University.

Park, Y. (2006) 'Sojourners to settlers: early constructions of Chinese identity in South Africa, 1879–1949', *African Studies*, 65(2): 201–31.

— (2008) 'State, myth, and agency in the construction of Chinese South African identities, 1948–1994', *Journal of Overseas Chinese*, 4(1): 69–90.

— (2009) 'Chinese migration in Africa', Occasional Paper, 24, China in Africa Project, Johannesburg: South African Institute of International Affairs.

— (2010) 'Boundaries, borders and borderland constructions: Chinese in contemporary South Africa and the region', *African Studies*, 69(3): 457–79.

Peck, J. and N. Theodore (2007) 'Variegated capitalism', *Progress in Human Geography*, 31(6): 731–72.

Phillips, M. (2006) 'G-7 to warn China over costly loans to poor countries', *Wall Street Journal*, 15 September, p. A2.

Phoenix, A. and P. Pattynama (2006) 'Intersectionality', *European Journal for Women's Studies*, 13: 187–92.

Pickles, J. and J. Woods (1989) 'Taiwanese investment in South Africa', *African Affairs*, 88(353): 507–28.

Portes, A. (1997) 'Globalization from below: the rise of transnational communities', Working Paper WPTC-98-01, ESRC Transnational Communities Project, www.transcomm.ox.ac.uk/working%20papers/portes.pdf (accessed 25 November 13).

Portes, A. and L. Jensen (1987) 'What's an ethnic enclave? The case for conceptual clarity', *American Sociological Review*, 52: 768–71.

Portes, A. and J. Sensenbrenner (1993)

'Embeddedness and immigration: notes on the social determinants of economic action', *American Journal of Sociology*, 98(6): 1320–50.

Power, M., G. Mohan and M. Tan-Mullins (2012) *Powering Development: China's Energy Diplomacy and Africa's Future*, London: Palgrave Macmillan.

Raine, S. (2009) *China's African Challenges*, London and New York: Routledge.

Rongji, Z. (2000) 'Strengthen solidarity, enhance co-operation and pursue common development', speech at the closing ceremony of FOCAC, Beijing, 12 October, www.focac.org/eng/wjjh/t404118.htm (accessed 16 June 2008).

Rosenberg, J. (2006) 'Why is there no international historical sociology?', *European Journal of International Relations*, 12(3): 307–40.

SAFPI (2012) 'FOCAC 2012: Sino-African partnership gains momentum', www.safpi.org/news/article/2012/focac-2012-sino-african-partnership-gains-momentum (accessed 28 November 2013).

Sautman, B. and Y. Hairong (2006) 'Honour and shame? China's Africa ties in comparative perspectives', in L. Wild and D. Mepham (eds), *The New Sinosphere: China in Africa*, London: Institute for Public Policy Research, pp. 54–61.

— (2007) 'Friends and interests: China's distinctive links with Africa', *African Studies Review*, 50(3): 75–114.

Sautman, B. and H. Yan (2009) 'African perspectives on China–Africa links', *China Quarterly*, 199: 728–59.

Scheld, S. (2010) 'The "China Challenge": the global dimensions of activism and the informal economy in Dakar, Senegal', in I. Lindell (ed.), *Africa's Informal Workers. Collective Agency, Alliances and Transnational Organizing in Urban Africa*, London: Zed Books.

— (2011) 'Racism, "free-trade" and consumer "protection": the controversy of Chinese petty-traders in Dakar, Senegal', in P. Hoikkala and D. Wills (eds), *Dimensions of International Migration*, Newcastle-upon-Tyne: Cambridge Scholars Publishing.

Schuman, H. and S. Presser (1996) *Questions and Answers in Attitude Surveys*, New York: Sage.

Servant, J.-C. (2005) 'Moscow and Beijing, Asia's roaring economies: China's trade safari in Africa', *Le Monde diplomatique*, http://monde-diplo.com/2005/05/11chinafrica (accessed 28 November 2013).

Shen, I. (2006) *A Century of Chinese Exclusion Abroad*, Beijing: Foreign Language Press.

Shen, S. (2009) 'A constructed (un)reality on China's re-entry into Africa: the Chinese online community perception of Africa (2006–2008), *Journal of Modern African Studies*, 47(3): 425–48.

Shen, S. and I. Taylor (2012) 'Ugandan youths' perceptions of relations with China', *Asian Perspective*, 36(4): 693–723.

Silvey, R. (2004) 'Power, difference and mobility: feminist advances in migration studies', *Progress in Human Geography*, 28(4): 490–506.

Skeldon, R. (2011) 'China: from exceptional case to global participant', www.migrationinformation.org/Profiles/display.cfm?ID=219 (accessed 28 November 2013).

Skinner, G. W. (1976) 'Mobility strategies in late imperial China: a regional systems analysis', in C. A. Smith (ed.), *Regional Analysis*, New York: Academic Press, pp. 327–64.

Snow, P. (1988) *The Star Raft: China's Encounter with Africa*, London: Weidenfeld and Nicolson.

— (1995) 'China and Africa: consensus and camouflage', in T. Robinson and D. Shambaugh (eds), *Chinese Foreign Policy: Theory and Practice*, Oxford: Oxford University Press.

Staehle, S. (2007) 'How to integrate China into the global aid regime', paper presented at the conference 'China and Africa, who benefits?', Frankfurt, 14–15 December.

Takyi-Boadu, C. (2005) 'Ghana's retail trade under siege', *The Chronicle*, 9 November.

Taylor, I. (1998) 'China's foreign policy towards Africa in the 1990s', *Journal of Modern African Studies*, 36(3): 443–60.

— (2006a) 'China's oil diplomacy in Africa', *International Affairs*, 82(5): 937–59.

— (2006b) *China and Africa: Engagement and Compromise*, London: Routledge.

— (2007a) 'Governance in Africa and Sino-African relations: contradictions or confluence?', *Politics*, 27(3): 139–46.

— (2007b) 'China's relations with Nigeria', *The Round Table: The Commonwealth Journal of International Affairs*, 96(392): 631–45.

— (2009) *China's New Role in Africa*, Boulder, CO: Lynne Rienner.

Thuno, M. (2001) 'Reaching out and incorporating Chinese overseas: the trans-territorial scope of the PRC by the end of the 20th century', *The China Quarterly*, 168: 910–29.

Trofimov, Y. (2007) 'New management: in Africa China's expansion begins to stir resentment', *Wall Street Journal*, 2 February, p. A1.

Tsing, A. (2004) *Friction: An Ethnography of Global Connection*, Princeton, NJ: Princeton University Press.

Tung, W. L. (1974) *The Chinese in America 1820–1973: A Chronology and Fact Book*, New York: Oceana Publications.

UN (2007) United Nations Conference on Trade and Development, *Asian Foreign Direct Investment in Africa: Towards a New Era of Cooperation among Developing Countries*, New York: United Nations.

— (2012) 'Infrastructure strengthening the foundation for African's development' [Online]. Available at: http://www.unis.unvienna.org/pdf/MDG_Africa_infrastructure.pdf.

UPI (2013) 'China investments in Africa boom', www.upi.com/Business_News/2013/03/20/China-investments-in-Africa-boom/UPI-68541363778204 (accessed 28 November 2013).

Utomi, P. (2008) *China and Nigeria*, Washington, DC: Center for Strategic and International Studies.

Valentine, G. (2007) 'Theorising and researching intersectionality: a challenge for feminist geography', *Professional Geographer*, 59: 10–21.

Van Hear, N., N. Bakewell and K. Long (2012) 'Drivers of migration, migrating out of poverty research programme consortium', Working paper 1, University of Sussex.

Vertovec, S. and R. Cohen (2002) 'Introduction: conceiving cosmopolitanism', in R. Vertovec and R. Cohen (eds), *Conceiving Cosmopolitanism: Theory, Context, and Practice*, Oxford: Oxford University Press, pp. 1–22.

Waldron, A. (2003) *From War to Nationalism: China's Turning Point, 1924–1925*, Cambridge: Cambridge University Press.

Watts, M. (1994) 'Oil as money: the devil's excrement and the spectacle of black gold', in S. Corbridge, R. Martin and N. Thrift (eds), *Money, Space and Power*, Oxford: Blackwell, pp. 406–45.

Weidenbaum, M. (1996) 'The Chinese family business enterprise', *California Management Review*, 38(4): 141–56.

Weinstein, W. (ed.) (1975) *Chinese and Soviet Aid to Africa*, New York and London: Praeger.

Wilhelm, J. (2006) 'The Chinese communities in South Africa', in S. Buhlungu, J. Daniel, R. Southall and J. Lutchman (eds), *State of the Nation: South Africa 2005–2006*, Cape Town: HSRC Press, pp. 350–68.

Williams, P. F. and Y. Wu (2004) *The Great Wall of Confinement: The Chinese Prison Camp Through Contemporary Fiction and Reportage*, Los Angeles, CA: University of California Press.

Wong, M. (2006) 'Chinese workers in the garment industry in Africa: implications of the contract labour dispatch system on the international labour movement', *Labour, Capital and Society*, 39(1): 69–111.

World Bank (2013) *The Africa Competitiveness Report 2013*, www3.weforum.org/docs/WEF_Africa_Competitiveness_Report_2013.pdf (accessed 28 November 2013).

WSWS (2002) 'Nigerian factory fire kills 45 workers', *World Socialist Web Site*, 25 September, www.wsws.org/articles/2002/sep2002/fire-s25.shtml (accessed 27 March 2011).

Xinhua (2011) 'China's foreign aid', http://news.xinhuanet.com/english2010/china/2011-04/21/c_13839683.htm (accessed 4 February 2014).

Yan, H. and B. Sautman (2013) '"The beginning of a world empire"? Contesting the discourse of Chinese copper mining in Zambia', *Modern China*, 39: 131–64.

Yang, G. (2003) 'The internet and civil society in China: a preliminary assessment', *Journal of Contemporary China*, 12(3): 453–75.

Yap, M. and D. L. Man (1998) *Colour, Confusion and Concession*, Hong Kong: Hong Kong University Press.

Young, N. and J. Shih (2003) *The Chinese*

Diaspora and Philanthropy, Harvard Global Equity Initiative, www.issuelab.org/resource/chinese_diaspora_and_philanthropy (accessed 28 November).

Yuval-Davis, N. (2006) 'Intersectionality and feminist politics', *European Journal of Women's Studies*, August, 13(3): 193–209.

Zhang, W. and S. Wang (2005) Overseas Chinese Affairs Office of the State Council, CCP, PRC. Adapted and translated from W. Zhang, '*HuaJiao-HuaRenGaiShu*' (Overseas Chinese Brief), *Overseas Chinese in Africa*, pp. 215–35.

— (2010) 'Migration and trade: the role of Overseas Chinese in economic relations between China and Southeast Asia', *International Journal of China Studies*, 1(1): 174–93.

Zhu, Y. (2006) *Migration and the Development of Sending Areas: Evidence from China and Ensuring Research Issues*, paper presented to the Institution for Future Studies international workshop on Strengthening Research Capacities to Enhance the Benefits of Migration for Development, Stockholm, 12 June.

Zukin, S. and P. DiMaggio (1990) 'Introduction', in S. Zukin and P. DiMaggio (eds), *Structures of Capital: The Social Organization of the Economy*, Cambridge: Cambridge University Press, pp. 1–36.

INDEX